THE HIGHEST COMMON DENOMINATOR

ROGER OBANDO

ISBN: 978-0-578-61034-4

Printed in the United States of America.

First printing edition 2019.

For media inquiries, please email:
media@rogerobando.com

"The worst form of inequality is to try and make unequal things equal."

-Aristotle

DEDICATION

To my parents. Thanks to your sacrifice, your American dream has become my American reality.

A FOREWARD
BY RICKY WILLIAMS

Ricky Williams is an American former football running back who played 12 seasons in the National Football League and one season in the Canadian Football League. He played college football for the University of Texas, where he was a two-time All-American and won the Heisman Trophy. He is now the esteemed founder of Real Wellness.

What is your story? How did it shape you? Did you write it? Will you? We are all the authors of our choices, and for some of us, those choices led us to pursue paths that are not often taken. For others, circumstances led us on journeys that didn't align with what is accepted by society. But life happens, and we have to make sure that we always calibrate towards a more authentic end. For me, the journey to health has been one that I've attempted my entire life, from a high school injury to a professional football career that took its physical toll, I have searched for healing. True Wellness. Real Wellness.

My idea of health has evolved over the years. As a young professional athlete, I defined health as being strong enough to do my job well. That attitude led to tremendous success in football, but my limited idea of health prevented me from experiencing the same kind of success in my personal and spiritual life. As those facets started to crumble, they caught my attention, and I began to prioritize my relationship with myself. Most importantly, I learned what was needed for me to stay healthy. I learned that I needed to keep an open mind and then share my understandings with those who were also on a path of education. I learned that I needed to be using what I know to help people feel better. I learned the importance of listening to my body and responding to its needs.

This information about myself led to pursue a study of yoga, meditation, and a variety of holistic healing modalities, including Ayurveda and traditional Chinese medicine. And so, I have now made understanding and cultivating health my life. My health routine consists of a daily habit of checking in with my heart, mind, and body and doing what I can to keep them communicating. It is when this internal dialogue stops, that disease tends to prevail.

I learned that diversity of options is diversity of self-to empower ourselves to pursue health, we are obligated to pursue open choices that lead us there. The best self is the one that we choose - whether we focus on health, career, or our selves - the elevation is a result of our choosing.

In my journey, that choice meant reaching beyond the community to cannabis.

My understanding of the cannabis industry is based on my experiences. I came to the industry when I was invited to speak on a panel at a regional conference in 2015, and the magnitude of the power of cannabis awed me. I've seen the industry grow tremendously since then, not only the legislative changes and the subsequent opening of more markets, but also growth in sophistication and intellectual diversity. I've seen what often felt like the 'Wild, Wild West' start to mature into something that is headed rapidly into the mainstream. From there, i consorted with diverse minds that search for growth, for exposure, and for choice. I found the best of people, of innovation, and of health.

To me, that is the power of a strong, diverse, and empowering community. And that is why I created Real Wellness. It was born to serve the growing fascination with cannabis as medicine to open people's minds to a different model of health and healing. One that recognizes the value of both plant medicinal and altered states. To promote the idea that real wellness can be facilitated by and with the conscious use of cannabis. We aim to educate and empower people to take their health and wellness into their own hands. Our intention to expand beyond the space is to feed the minds and hearts which are being opened by cannabis. Elemental to my story is that cannabis can open minds, but it's up to us to do something with the opening.

Roger embodies that opening. He creates choice, and then rises with his community, adding others to his growth. The synergy of his impact is that while we rise in service of wellness in all aspects, from personal to professional, we take others in our circle along. His passion for finding a higher common ground is the future, and the soul of cannabis.

I envision the cannabis industry as maintaining its soul as it comes into maturity. What I mean is that the soul of cannabis, I believe, is reflected in the counter-culture that serves as its conduit into its final form. Sure, there is a lot of money to be made in this industry, but I believe far more importantly there are a lot of people who can benefit physically, psychologically and spiritually from the responsible use of cannabis. Part of the soul of cannabis is also related to the many people who have sacrificed so much for their role in allowing cannabis to become an industry.

I think the key to moving towards a more holistic social space is that we must do what we can to tell authentic and inspiring stories. Stories drive our understanding of the world, and compelling stories help us to create meaning. I know that sharing my story of being publicly criticized and professionally humiliated for my use of cannabis and my subsequent life path which led me to the cannabis industry has inspired people to appreciate the value of social diversity. So many stories about cannabis are either hyperbolic propaganda for or against it. I am especially proud of the founding story of Real Wellness. It represents for me a coming together of my talents, interests, and purpose. It's been so healing for me to find a way to integrate cannabis into my life this way. I believe more stories about how people are doing that need to be told.

Roger's story is one that we all share, because we all try and climb the heights of ourselves, and ascend into a better self.

True wellness starts with a story.

AUTHOR'S NOTE

You probably don't know who I am. And you probably don't know what I do. So why are you reading this book?

Let's walk through it together.

My name is Roger Obando, and I had every chance to fail. My story of a lower-middle-class life isn't atypical, but as the son of immigrants and a person of color, I faced a steeper climb to success. Normality, however, isn't a paved road, and I didn't want an ordinary existence - I thirsted for impact. I made a series of choices, sought options, and embraced the chaos of attempt.

So, now, I am a technologist. I've been a CTO and co-founder of numerous companies for close to twenty years after graduating from Duke University, with a degree in Computer Science, and surprising to many, a minor in Art.

My life is a series of interactions that I leveraged to elevate my ideas. I want to say that I designed every circumstance, but that isn't how life unravels. So, what I will say is that I designed what I wanted in life, and took advantage of every opportunity that would lead me there.

It led me to cannabis, and now, to advocacy.

We can all create our own future, but like us, it morphs. It grows, it iterates, and it evolves. When you reach the peak of success, you have to start over, redefine, and renew. Success is a moving target.

So why should you read what I have to say?

Because reconciling technology into the cannabis market gave me an insight into what this industry really means to our social constructs, to the concept of entrepreneurialism and risk, and perhaps most critically, to how we empower ourselves to reach, apply, and grow.

Because connecting ideas means retrofitting lessons.

Because life is a series of interactions.

Leveraging our intersections in search of our best self is a shared goal.

I hope that by sharing my experiences, our ideas will align at the highest level, in service of opportunity, access, and success.

CONTEXTUALIZING CANNABIS

Cause and effect.

Everything starts with an origin story. Cannabis is no different. It starts with potential, and thankfully, ends there as well.

Cannabis is a phoenix. It has burned, yet risen. So too, have the people and industries that have arisen around it.

The criminality assigned to cannabis is a historic epidemic of misinformation. The control that monopolies exert onto social constructs, and how entire segments of our nation's fabric have been subjugated, institutionalized, and unempowered is a stain on our world.

But like all stories that began with good intentions, the base traits of greed, manipulation, and control, forced our social systems into a canal that deprived farmers, patients, and minorities of the opportunities to not only participate in, or at the least not suffer so disproportionately from, the wrongful criminalization of the plant.

Every action has an equal and opposite reaction.

The origin story of cannabis is shockingly awful. The anti-cannabis movement that began in the early 1900's, and rapidly accelerated in the mid-1930's, is mired in racism that persists today.

From the prohibition of alcohol to the ultimate criminalization of cannabis, politicians painted the plant, and the communities who used or grew it, as a threat to the Evangelical way of life. With the financial and press support of oligarchs like William Hearst, the Marijuana (a term that is, shockingly, not derived from the Spanish culture), Tax Act of 1937, fundamentally altered the potential of the industry, crippling, choking, and criminalizing anybody who touched it.

Yet the proliferation of the law - as all laws designed to constrict option and progress - adversely affected the lowest tiers of society. The same levels that were barely eeking their out of segregation, lack of representation, and an utter lack of opportunity to make a living. At every juncture, their freedom shrunk as cannabis became an illicit drug that seeped into their streets, their records, and their futures.

For decades, our country solved for the War on Drugs by imprisoning - en masse - hundreds of thousands of minorities for their supposed crimes, essentially shackling them with the 1971 Controlled Substances Act.

Right on schedule, it was a Schedule One, and cannabis become public enemy number one.

So too, did minorities.

In the span of a few decades, the proliferation of social perceptions, legislative enforcement, and profoundly misinformed propaganda fundamentally altered the trajectory of minority groups, growers, and small businesses who simply wanted an opportunity to do well in life.

It is critical to understand this.

Generations of intelligent, hardworking, deserving, and most importantly, INNOCENT people - left with one of two inhuman options: either live as a criminal, or live behind bars.

Without options, there is no freedom.

The criminalization of cannabis led to the continued criminalization of color.

Green dollars. Green greed. Green plant.

But a black stain on our history.

So why cannabis?

I, like so many others, fell into it.

Once there, statistics became people.

Criminals became fathers.

The truth emerged.

As legalization efforts spread, so too did understandings.

When the industry went from illegal to medically, and then recreationally, legal in certain states, the effect was immediate.

Legislators became investors. Repeat offenders - (see: growers) - became farmers. Color became powerful.

I saw a chance to put a megaphone to the opportunities I saw ahead of me, and everyone whose prison doors had opened. Those that had been systematically underserved and imprisoned had to emerge into the harsh light of a market that didn't have the infrastructure to support it.

What could I do? What could I do in service to those whose opportunities had been stolen? How could we create connections between the past misgivings and the future possibilities?

Solutions were simply adaptations. By recognizing that new consumers were evolving from old mindsets, the industry had to simultaneously battle profoundly negative perceptions while providing potent and progressive solutions. Marketing the product became an industry in and of itself.

This is where I met cannabis. When my skills could serve liberty, and growth, and optionality, I found a space to call home.

Here, my color was nothing more than that. It didn't help, but more importantly, it didn't hurt. The industry is naturally empathetic because everyone risked everything to build, sustain, and grow it. There were no arbitrary dividers designed to divide and conquer.

Cannabis was, and is, about community. The solutions engineered had a singular mission: empower everyone. At least, give them a choice.

THE ORIGINS
OF BAKER

I question everything.

Everything is worth understanding.

From understanding comes insight, and from there, action.

Right intention, right consequence.

It was late 2014 when myself and my co-founders had recently decided that we were not going to build native apps for smartphones (for those who are already lost, this means an app like any other you'd open on your Android or iPhone). Instead, we had decided (well I, as the CTO, had strongly suggested) that we build a mobile web app that could be accessed through the browser on our customers' smartphones. As a startup with next to no financial resources, this made the most sense for a few reasons.

Number one, we could develop a single product that would work across the entire ecosystem of smartphones. Had we chosen the alternative, we would have to create and maintain two products (for those keeping score that means about one hundred percent more work). As the only developer on the team, the responsibility of my suggestion fell squarely on my shoulders, and as such, stole sleep and replaced it with permanent solutions, some of which I considered. As one of the founders of the company, this made dollar signs dance across my vision and not in a good way. Had we built a native app, it would have been twice as much work and cost about the same factor of expense - it just wasn't tenable.

Secondly, I had been developing for the web for close to twenty years. I could do this with my eyes closed. The alternative would have required much more trial and error, which would make the development process much slower, and we didn't have time to waste. We knew that we needed to get our new online ordering product – the yet unnamed Baker Technologies - designed to serve the rapidly expanding cannabis industry to market, as soon as possible.

Last on our list, and perhaps the item most contingent on an uncontrollable variable, we had to come to terms with the fact that we were creating a product that would allow people to order marijuana through the internet. Did we genuinely think we'd be able to sweet talk our way into the Apple Store? Most people don't realize that you can't just throw up any old app on the Apple Store and cross your fingers that people will download it. Every app on that marketplace needs to be vetted and approved by Apple – which is a rigorous and often-frustrating process - and even though Tim Cook and I are alumni of the same university, I didn't think that would be enough common ground for me to convince him to let me do this thing.

This was especially true at a time when our collective country still wasn't sure how they felt about the recently enacted legislation that allowed for the "legal" purchase of marijuana in Colorado and Washington. There were too many variables and risks for the monoliths of our nation to fully support our endeavors.

So, we navigated alone.

Nevertheless, we decided to forge ahead, but the obstacle that we knew we would inevitably face revealed itself. We knew that we needed to be able to communicate with the consumers that were going to be placing orders on our system. Email felt like a clunky touch point to interact, and had we been able to create native apps, we'd be able to use the now-ubiquitous push notification systems (you know, those little notices that tell you when somebody likes your Instagram photo or when you've got mail) to notify users of their order status and updates.

Unfortunately, that was outside the realm of possibilities.

Sometimes complicated problems require simple solutions.

"How about text messages?"

Suddenly, there was clarity, and I set off to feverishly code what would ultimately be our proof of concept that we would end up launching just five weeks later.

Necessity, we all agree, is the mother of invention. At the time, it seemed like a decision that was based purely on need. And it was. Twilio had only recently launched to provide SMS (that's text messaging for those who are curious. "Short message service" for the literal folks out there), as a service to developers, which meant we didn't have to build it from scratch. We could outsource the actual delivery of the messages to Twilio, which afforded us more time – which we desperately needed - to develop our core offering. The decision made sense no matter how you looked at it.

If it worked for Uber, it would work for us.

Fast forward nine months, and we developed a product that was working for a handful of beta clients in Colorado. Excited about the progress, we continue to add functionalities to the surprise and delight of our small customer base, while continuing to grow it by providing the most seamless and holistic experience possible.

"What if we allowed the customer to text back? Can we do that?"

Well. That was interesting.

Carter Davidson (our VP of Sales) and I fondly remember those early days of our startup, when you are "moving fast and breaking things." Carter would eagerly approach my desk and make a suggestion to add to the product what she gleaned would be a value-add with information she learned from one of our sales prospects. "If we could just add this feature, I can sign this client," I remember hearing on a reasonably regular basis.

The beauty of this stage of a company is that the answer was generally "yes." There were no enterprise clients with Service Level Agreements yet. Our clients knew that we were very early and they knew that they could expect some kinks in the system, but that after those issues were resolved, they would have an excellent product.

Another suggestion, another feature, and we set off to create a simple two-way text messaging system that would allow a customer to respond to the messages they received from their dispensary. They could suggest modifications to their orders or send a simple "thank you" and know that a budtender on the other end of the line would receive their message on the dashboard they were using to manage their orders.

Little did we know how much this one feature addition would impact the roadmap of our little company we had come together to start less than a year before.

Time went on, and we rapidly grew, in parallel to the market.

Close to a year later, we were in the middle of rolling out our latest product offering. Sometime in the previous twelve months we saw the writing on the wall for Colorado dispensaries - what once seemed like an endless pool of customers who wanted to come in and buy their cannabis (we had stopped using the word marijuana at this point,) products was dwindling and...of course they were. There was a new dispensary going up on what seemed to be every other corner. As new dispensaries opened, they would have "new client specials" aimed at acquiring new customers which thinned the herd of people lined up at most dispensary doors. As the customer base diluted, new stores with introductory deals were stealing loyal clients from pre-existing shops.

"Customer retention is our new initiative," somebody said. How can we prevent customers from leaving the dispensary they had been regularly frequenting? Loyalty programs were the obvious answer. We had recently seen systems like Fivestars and Belly make significant strides in coffee shops and restaurants. There was no reason why we couldn't build something similar for the cannabis market. Not only would this be a great way to stay ahead of the market, but it would be an innovative way for us to let the public know who WE were and what WE were doing in the industry. And so, we set off on creating, at first, digital loyalty programs for our online ordering products and eventually in-store tablets that mimicked the tablets people were used to interacting with at their local Starbucks.

"Simply enter your phone number on the tablet," a budtender would say, and a world of rewards was available at your fingertips.

And it worked. People were happy to enter their

details and receive information about how to get a pre-roll for a penny or a 10% discount on an edibles order. Eventually, we added the ability for the user to tell us a bit more about their preferred products. Did you like vape pens, edibles, topical lotions? We wanted to know.

With knowledge, comes insight.

Insight leads to transformation.

The proverbial light bulb had gone off in our collective head.

"What if we built a tool that would let the dispensary staff text their customers with tailored offerings by leveraging our data insights?"

At the time, dispensaries had minimal options for how to market to their customers. The de-facto method was to put ads in local papers. As you can imagine, it was challenging to quantify the return on investment on a print ad. As a function of the regulations surrounding the industry, they had to use very generic advertising to appeal to a wide array of people and generally the only way to incentivize users was to offer deep discounts that cut into a retailer's profits.

We immediately set off to create a tool that would allow dispensary owners to send text messages to their users with offers based on their purchase habits and product preferences. They could send specific deals to individuals who were most likely to take advantage of them, and you could track the efficacy of said messages.

Just like that, we were off to the races.

By the time we entered into a deal to merge with three other cannabis companies and eventually go public on the Canadian Securities Exchange (just twenty-four months or so later), in which our company was valued at over nine figures, we had acquired a market share of approximately 35% of the entire North American legal cannabis retail market. That meant that for every three legal dispensaries in North America, at least one of them was using Baker.

It still blows my mind to think about this.

Looking at the cannabis market now and seeing how many different software and service providers exist in the space, it may be easy to look at this story and dismiss it as something of no real significance.

But 2014 was the beginning of the beginning, and we were considered crazy. The industry at the time simply wasn't attracting entrepreneurs with this sort of vision and resilience. I would like to believe that the Baker team laid a lot of the groundwork for what the modern software and services segment of the cannabis industry looks like. I'll always be proud of what we built, but I think as time moves on I'll be prouder of the doors we opened for other entrepreneurs who didn't know how much opportunity existed in this space. It is often said that the first through the wall are the bloodiest, and I can attest to this, but I wouldn't change a thing about what we did and when we decided to do it.

So, when I say that our belief had an impact, and helped light the industry on fire, I say it with the full knowledge of the effort and tenacity it took to build despite the odds.

We leveled up. And so too should you. There is opportunity everywhere.

PROLOGUE

From my youth, I have been driven.
Predestined paths didn't align with my understanding of
the world, so I chose to follow my own.
My immigrant parents pushed the boundaries of thinking
beyond their comfort zone, and I followed suit. Why not
challenge the status quo? And so, I did. From my choice
of education to my choice of career, to my intentional
behavior as a leader, I pushed beyond the acceptable. I
pushed then, and I push now, because if we don't push
forward, we don't transform.

***

I am fascinated by transformation. Inputs that determine outputs; responses instead of reactions; our reality versus our desire.

We are told that we are products of our environment.

I think we can produce our environment, and that mindset is the key to our evolution.

Evolution is the response of our environment shaping us, but in our personal evolution, is it possible that we can begin to shape our environment?

Perhaps if we reorganize our perspective from one of reaction to one of intentionality, we can begin to alter the landscape of our reality.

In my experience, life is a calculated rearrangement of circumstance, and it is up to us to convert the baser self into a product of value. We start small, transforming nothing into something. We begin with the base, and then we are left to decide what values to add and subtract to evolve.

Someone once told me that this is like the art of alchemy--to take a base metal and break it down in order to transform it into a precious metal; something that the market values. The goal of any transformation is ultimately optimization. Optimization leads to optionality. Optionality leads to a higher version of yourself by allowing for access to more opportunity. And opportunity sits at the top of the totem pole. If we are not born at the top of the pole, we have to make our way up.

Some of us have to climb more than others-- proof that our slates are not blank. We are all born into circumstances; circumstances that define our data sets, our functions, our calculations. Wealth or poverty. White or Black. Immigrant or native. Religious or atheist.

We can stay on the path assigned to us, with A/B choices that leave little room for growth or autonomy or divergence from our pre-ordained ceilings. Or we can create our own optionality, seeking to go beyond the borders of the cultural and societal expectations set out for us.

Sometimes, those expectations are reflections of our own capabilities.

To grow, however, those must be challenged.

As humans, we put ourselves and others into categories. These categories are based on gross generalizations, and yet they usher us, like cattle, to different sides of the fence. The group in which we are placed dictates what we have access to -- money, education, ideas, people -- simply, what we can and cannot achieve.

These are arbitrary restraints, and in many ways, can be as real as you allow them to be, but the point remains. They are designed to keep society segmented by status, or color, or education. These limits can be socially or self-imposed. If we are not careful, these limits can define our outcomes.

The sum of these constraints, or definitions, equate to a tribe - that group to which you were born, or belong, or mirror, at least on the surface.

This is why it is so important to recognize that your tribe is part of you, but you are not your tribe. You are you. And you are capable of defining your own limits. You can, should, and must characterize yourself.

Of course, you are, in part, defined by experiences. However, your circumstances do not need to define your metrics of success. Your beginning does not determine your ending. Why? Because your end has not been solved for. Your ending is a function of 'x' – a variable of your choice, your focus, your design. You get to write it however you wish.

Too often we allow the conditions into which we are born dictate our future; and if we do 'succeed' it is by society's definition of success, not our own. Too often, we live the life that is considered normal for our circumstance, and we fail to realize that circumstance is simply a condition, not a factor in our success.

Success is a personal definition.

If we are born into a particular gender, or skin color, or zip code, then we are statistically programmed for lesser opportunity. We are socialized to curb our ambitions based on our realities. We are designed to limit our potential on the probability of our success. We are told that what is acceptable is not a function of what is possible; it is a function of what is expected. We are told what is considered a sum of possible values (options) is based on the variables (traits).

I challenge anyone to name an underserved segment of society who are not fighting an uphill battle. In our society, we might generalize these segments by gender, or race, or socioeconomic status. Unfortunately, this might be one of the main issues with our society - that it is so easy to identify these groups. These battles are not ones that they asked for. They are struggling to achieve the most rudimentary of baselines to establish themselves as pseudo-relevant players in the game of life. If they want to be successful, they have to do more - much more, and in almost every vertical - from accessing education, hell, even books; to changing their names to sound less ethnic; to trying to learn how to register for the SAT's. It is difficult all day, in every way, to get to normal. Normality, let alone success is almost impossible to conceive.

There is no sugar coating this. It is the reality for the majority of people who fall into this category, myself included. (Notice that I said majority here. I am not generalizing - which is intentional and essential, because there are exceptions to all norms. Although there are obvious deviances from this experience, they are too few to register).

My bottom line was that I had to do more to get where I wanted to go. I may never know the root of this desire to stretch beyond my means. The only thing I can say is that it was an inherent feeling, a need to expand beyond the restraints of my community. It was a want and a requirement that I could not deny.

I have resolved that sometimes we just rise for reasons that we cannot comprehend. We rise because of something deep inside of us. Something that cannot be taught, something so inherently intrinsic that it is the difference between advancing or falling – motivation. And what is motivation? Motivation is a result of the intersection between conscious and unconscious desires.

The fusion from this intersection creates the contagious energy that is ambition.

Ambition, then, is a propeller.

For some, motivation comes from external factors. For others, it is more internal - generated from the self. External factors, such as our community or our status, can influence our desires, which in turn influence our actions. Sometimes we feel like we have something to prove, so we walk around with self-inflicted chips on our shoulders. Sometimes we feel like we have to do something in order to show that we can add value to society. Why? Because we feel "less than" - less than our peers or our potential, or because we do not fit the mold. So, we think that we need to show the world that we are something or that we can be something. This is especially true for immigrant children, kids who believe that because of their label they have to prove that they are even worth living.

Given fewer resources, we are expected to do more. Proof of self-worth then becomes the main qualifier of success.

We don't celebrate the immigrant who creates jobs or choose to become an entrepreneur instead of a blue-collar worker. Why? Because the mentality that faces those who haven't been born into success, or the United States, or have been validated by society, is that the least an immigrant can do, or that a first-generation child can do, is succeed. We are expected to become self-sufficient, or even successful, as our price to stay in this nation. It is a disproportionate lopsided expectation that the price immigrants and their families must pay for daring to exist in the U.S, is uncelebrated contributions.

We have to earn our keep.

Which, ironically, isn't a big motivator.

True motivation is self-engineered and self-propagated. Anecdotes aside, and with them, clichés, the truth is that our only option is not to find our place but to forge it. We can strike while the iron is hot, or make the iron hot by striking. For all intents and purposes, creating a path in life is a combination of your personal needs and desires colliding. When our natural inclination leads us to make choices that propel us forward, we align our desires, our tenacity, and our goals.

It isn't easy, and there is little if any, scaffolding around it.

I had every opportunity to fail. I was the child of immigrants who struggled to provide but did so anyhow. Many peers succumbed to the societal conditions that polluted our masses and suffered the consequences of bad luck mixed with bad choices.

For whatever reason, an oxygen mask kept me protected against the realities of circumstance; I pushed beyond the realities of my situation, and I became single-minded in my vision of success. I was single-minded in what I felt life could be - I was analytical, practical, and ambitious. Maybe it was because I never felt deprived, or perhaps it was because of the values my parents instilled into me. They never told me that I had limits; they stood beside me as I reached higher. Because of their support, my life, which I consider to be "normal" is far from their normal. The truth is, from a young age, my visions did not match those of my community; the normal I envisioned was unfathomable to many in my community.

I grew up in an "underserved community" in a region where "more" was not much. It was forgotten by those who could. I was "given" opportunities – namely, programs designed to celebrate my race - as a deciding factor in who I would become. Seminars, workbooks, and motivational courses infiltrated my impressionable mind, with statements that ensured that I knew my race was the reason I was receiving this information, and with that mindset, I was left to my own devices. Left to my own devices, I learned that understanding leads to opportunity. From experience, I learned that opportunity leads to wealth, not riches.

The way to move forward, I was taught, was to leverage my base traits – the color of my skin, the nature of my upbringing, even the region in which I lived.

I was taught to think that leveraging my heritage was

the singular launch pad of finding success.

I was taught that thinking low was taking the high road.

It seems that my thoughts, however, were always trying to elevate themselves.

Throughout my life and my career choices, I climbed the proverbial ladder, reaching upwards in search of a more fulfilling life.

I was headed to a higher place, but it was a journey without a map. In Denver, I was not only at a higher elevation; I was in a more heightened state of mind. What I did not realize was that in this city, I would help to write the underdog story of cannabis. I did not realize that the platform we worked to build would help bring cannabis into the light. I did not know that our technology would be a vector to begin the process of shifting the public's perception of the plant.

My journey, like that of cannabis, has been a matter of seeking to reach my potential while squashing the stigma along the way.

Stigmas are perceptions based on what we see and what we hear, which influences what we know. Sometimes, a matter of shifting a shame is a matter of modifying the image.

To go higher, I engineered my optics; looking in the mirror, I decided not just what success looks like to me but what I needed to achieve it – to climb the ladder so to speak. I shed my casual New Jersey accent and spoke intentionally, calculating my syntax. I want to make an obvious point here, however. I will refer to my good friend, Rico, whose personal experience cannot be better stated: "Without touching upon white supremacy and systemic discrimination's watering down of our nation's dialectal wealth...I truly wish code-switching didn't have to be a thing. We should be able to celebrate the diversity of our origins completely. My success shouldn't be tethered to my ability to 'speak so eloquently... like Obama!' But this is our reality, and so we adjust." It was, and is, an unfortunate reality that we contend with, but in service of focus, we adapt. I picked my clothes carefully, dressing for my desired part. I attended Duke University. I deliberately surrounded myself with circles of people that would attempt to achieve our shared definition of success. We were equally motivated to attain what we did not inherit - a life of continued opportunity.

We all make sacrifices. What we choose to give up, opens the door for what we can obtain.

I didn't want to survive. I wanted to thrive, and so I curated a life based on ideals, not on realities. The former, I could shape. The latter was set in stone.

"Man cannot remake himself without suffering, for he is both marble and sculptor." - Alexis Carrel

To reveal myself, I needed to chip away those elements that did not serve my needs.

Like everyone else in the world, the growing pains hurt. It is hard to look in the mirror and realize that parts of what is reflected, is no longer beneficial to your future self.

It is hard to create an identity.

And so, I sought to seek the best in myself, and others. I realized that despite divorcing myself from my tribe, we could not walk alone. Others whom I met along the way became peers on the journey and provided insights that I could not see for myself. We all tried to climb the ladder for a better life.

I found that achieving success was a matter of leveraging the highest shared traits, not the lowest.

I intersected only where I could learn, evolve, and grow.

I found that self-propagation was a matter of willful transformation.

I looked for the highest common denominator in every interaction.

I looked higher.

I found a community.

We found cannabis.

And together, we lit it on fire.

CHAPTER 1

REACH HIGHER

It is a creed that demands a commitment to a cause that reaches beyond the self. It is an elevation that serves the underserved, whose systematic under-representation has coerced them into the underdogs of life. The odds are not in their favor. Nor were the odds for cannabis, but the game isn't over.

I was not expected to thrive. I was created to survive, albeit well enough that I would not feel a lack. But to reach above a level I didn't know was a limit, I kept climbing, because I knew that there was more to my potential than I was allowed to.

Cannabis was not designed to succeed. In fact, every impediment to its success was fostered by the stakeholders of ignorance to ensure that it failed. But it is tenacious, and found a way to reach higher. Its birth as a modern mega-industry is the result of diverse minds and experiences.

It was built to succeed by those who believed in its potency. Through the efforts of many, it has emerged as an industry that leads with diversity, and evolved from reefer madness to an empowering choice.

To live by the creed that demands an elevated mindset I looked no further than cannabis.

***

Elements are composed of atoms, the most basic units of known existence - seemingly nonliving and yet full of life. Their actions are dictated by properties and charges that allow them to bind to other atoms. But interestingly, atoms connect based on their differences. Opposite charges combine to create compounds, compounds that become larger and stronger than they were before. Sometimes, the bonds within these compounds become so strong that the only way to break them into their baser parts is with an explosion – a supernova - proof that the compound existed, that it was something - that the "whole" that was created was stronger than the sum of its parts.

The process, the shifting and combining of particles to create something better, to create an idea or product that has never existed before, is called the art of alchemy. I am not comparing alchemy to science, merely deriving a metaphor.

The purity of empirical science is critical to an open mind that can entertain an idea without accepting it. Unlike science, alchemy required a suspension of disbelief, but an acceptance of magic. Alchemy, then, was art, and alchemists were much like entrepreneurs - taking an idea and growing it to epic proportions. It was, and is, hope mixed with passion with a dose of desperation.

Our modern version of alchemy has also transformed.

It is now the art of life, of creating yourself. This is the art of rising beyond the base to create that which had never existed before, transformed into something higher.

But how? How do you get to this point where your life becomes precisely what you want it to be? How do you reconcile your dreams with your reality? There must be some part, some element inside that strives to grow beyond the border of your reality or mind, and this is the fuel to generate that journey.

To start your journey to your goals, you will question every part of yourself, and what made you - your circle, your schooling, and your societal influences - and you will create a baseline sense of who you are. From there, you will build, trait by trait, and event by event, an end-goal version of your life. You will continue to rise, as you challenge the very socialization biases that built you, as you now rebuild yourself. You will question every moment of this journey - 'Am I capable?', 'Do they see through me?', 'Do I deserve this?' - but don't stop building. Every stone of self-doubt that is thrown your way is your opportunity for growth - collect them, and build your dream. To go higher, you will intersect at the highest common denominator.

The what, you may ask?

The highest common denominator, or as you will see me refer to it throughout this text, the HCD. It sounds familiar, right? Like a term that closely mimics one that was thrown around in your fourth-grade classroom: the greatest common divisor. While the HCD is a play on the word, it is also so much more. Let me explain why.

As you may or may not recall, the greatest common divisor is the "largest positive integer that evenly divides two or more integers." For example, the greatest common divisor of eight and twelve is four. The numbers eight and twelve are also divisible by the number two; however, two is not the highest nor the greatest number, it is one of the potential numbers that can divide into both eight and twelve. Therefore, four emerges as the greatest common divisor. Now, just like in life, there are conditions that must be met to find the greatest common divisor; there must be two or more integers involved, and these integers cannot equal zero. Now, how does this relate to the HCD? Well, to intersect at the HCD, you need two or more people, and both must be willing to bring something to the table.

By now you are probably wondering, Roger, why are you giving me a math lesson? And I want you to know that my intention is not to fill the shoes of your elementary school math teacher but rather to use a mathematical concept to define a principle that has characterized my success. To me, the highest common denominator is the most sophisticated point of intersection between two or more people. These intersections occur in our daily lives, through work, conversations, or even introductions. They are exposures that add to the clarity of our picture and allow for iterations in our image to develop.

Let's assume for a moment that alchemy is real and that I am an alchemist who is capable of turning lead to gold. Elevation of my base ideas and capabilities is the tool that I would use to transform my life, to create what I want despite the odds set before me as a function of my culture, my low socioeconomic status, or where I grew up. I mean really, how do you get to an elevated place when you don't have the same access that other people do? You start at the bottom. And then, you level up. You choose to get where you want to go, and you coerce yourself to achieve more than is expected of you.

The keyword here is "you." You do this. No one else does this for you. You have to have the awareness and the willingness to transcend expectation and curate your outcome.

I was able to create my own success because I always sought to level up; I said "yes" to opportunity. I rearranged all of the necessary parts to create my final product. I chose to leverage my culture, my knowledge, my values, and my skill-set in nearly every meaningful encounter. I could have let my tribe dictate these factors, but instead, I used them to my benefit, not my deficit. I urge everyone to do the same: don't let obstacles subtract from your self - transform them into additives that build you up. Each time I intersected or conversed with someone, I did so in the most sophisticated way possible, because I knew, and know that when I am at my best, I attract the best. I do so at the HCD.

I want to be clear; I am not a fan of social climbing. I believe that it is inauthentic and ultimately (and something which should be of your most pressing concern), it does not allow for internal growth. I believe in elevation by paying your dues. Every step requires sweat and study. If you want to walk uphill, hydrate. Replenish yourself with new ideas, self-support, and confidence. In doing so, you will meet many others who are also on their own journeys, but at different places along the way. Meeting at the highest level, both for yourself and others, should be an organic event, not a conspiracy of trying to jump rungs on the ladder if you aren't ready. I did not design who I wanted to meet. I was not trying to be something. I designed myself so that people would want to meet me. I developed a life and went about living it.

The beginning of every journey starts with a step. In my case, it began with a choice to reach for more than I had or rather, more than was expected of me. Once I chose to obtain my definition of success, I took the steps necessary to get there – these steps included high-level interactions and intersections. Each one allowed me to take another step up on the totem pole. I had to climb in order to reach the heights that I desired, and when you are climbing, you have no choice but to pick the move that will help you to rise, the one that even after you make it offers you some sort of opportunity.

With each upward step, I gained something that I could use to get to the next level. Intersections in my life became like a video game. To get to the next level, I had to collect something. Once I got what I needed, I could start again. This process repeated itself until, against the odds set against me, I ended up where I wanted to be.

To climb in the entrepreneurial world, you have to play the part. So, I designed myself for success-- methodically, pragmatically, and wholly. In the recent world of quantifying success, "exits" are our barometers – when, how much, valuation and the rest. Rather than qualifying our success as a function of our experience, growth, or contributions, we often wait, impatiently and with expectations, for the day of our first public offering. At 40 years old, after 20 years of grinding, and learning, and failing, and growing, industry awarded me with a title few receive – a technologist with a successful exit.

But the means to the end were more formative, and more pertinent to my market value than a successful exit determined.

So, I'll start at the beginning of my end – Baker Technologies.

It wasn't entirely fate that created one of the most successful software platforms in cannabis – it was pragmatism coupled with opportunity. From the moment of our initial meeting, my co-founders - Joel and David – and I found a synergy between our skill-sets, which we continued to leverage in the conception, iterations, pivots, evolution, and final platform that is now being used at thousands of dispensaries across legalized markets

By setting a baseline, we elevated the optics, interactions, and experience of our industry.

We started Baker because we identified a problem in need of a solution. Namely, how cannabis could be accessed, used, and optimized to an increasingly massive legalized audience.

A mile high, in the mile-high city. It was Colorado that welcomed our coastal experience, but adapting to our perception of the problem (a rapidly expanding market base) versus the actual problem (how to access this market base while combatting societal biases, inter-industry demands, and federal optics), was a balancing act that required a significant level of constant introspection, pivoting, and focus.

To determine the viability of the problem, then, we observed the standard operating procedures of how the industry functioned, what the stakeholders required, how our user base was growing, and most importantly, which segments of the market would benefit from our product.

We didn't denigrate our passion in this formula, however. Entering this Wild West of an industry in the early days of legalization required a deep desire – personal experience, a respect for the liberty that the plant allowed users in their wellness needs, or simply because we recognized a disruptive market opportunity.

That desire, as all successful entrepreneurial passions are built on, must be tempered with respect for empirical data – data that doesn't sugarcoat opportunity with bias, belief, or desires. In the case of Baker, we continuously measured the temperature of our market, pivoting to maximize potentials, reduce variables, and most importantly, serve our users.

To broaden our base, we need to sharpen our focus.

Expanding your network, scope of knowledge, or even your possibilities in life requires a single-mindedness in achieving your goal. So, learn what your skills are and leverage them.

We played to our strengths - extrapolating an ideas' most potent potential by bringing it to mass market – an industry that was sustained, deep underground, by passionate stewards of the plant – now needed to emerge, rise and see the light.

Minds from every walk of life wanted to interact, in any way, as the industry burgeoned. We made it our mission to seek talent that was based on three qualifiers – experience, drive, and tenacity.

To do that, we expanded the scope of what a successful company looked like. The spectrum that was illuminated continues to be astounding. My own heritage was critical to this focus on inclusion. I knew firsthand that surrounding yourself with those whose only shared traits are culture and background doesn't create a complete team – we must align ourselves with those who share a similar mindset.

The greatest equalizer in opportunity is simple: a shared level of passion, dedication, and hunger.

That is the difference between dreaming and doing.

We diversified, transcending the concept that diversity is solely a representation of cultural backgrounds, race, or gender. We formed a powerful team of men and women with varied cultural and ideological ties.

We found value in our diversity and expanded to inconceivable heights because of it. Too often businesses are run and dominated by the people who have been the gatekeepers of opportunity — those born into the right conditions, primed for success; those who do not need to look outside of their community to gain the footholds needed to succeed. The reality is, diversity creates a complex and highly functional ecosystem. It adds varying viewpoints, experiences, and beliefs – all of which convert to a stronger, more marketable and universal product. If we stay within our tribe, we will only know that which our tribe teaches. We cannot grow if we do not go outside of the matrix of what we know.

As Baker grew, I often thought about my end game, the much revered, almost elusive exit from the product of my passion and sacrifice. My exit, much like all of the other decisions in my life, was calculated. My departure was an opportunity to leave on a high note; to go when I knew that the end would lead to another beginning.

So often, we look at opportunities, and we leap without thinking. Prospects are enticing, especially when what you have always wanted is dangled in front of you. But, you must ask yourself, is this the best opportunity? To understand the answer, you must weigh the risk, calculate it, and explore the pathways that form as a result of leaping.

And as you move forward, do not worry about leaving a legacy, worry about picking up an opportunity. Fame and fortune may seem alluring, but they should not be the fruits that you try to grab. Your goal should be to say "yes" to circumstances that heighten the possibility of you attaining success. Fame and fortune can be a byproduct of this, but they should not be the ultimate goal.

2014, and my first exposure into the cannabis

industry, not as a consumer, but as a professional, in every way, sparked my curiosity. I was no longer surrounded by the monotone colors of typical "big business" environments. There were shades of everything – people, ideas, legalities, and uses. Early in the transition to legalization, conversations moved from underground grows to brightly lit conference rooms.

But the industry was still finding its legs.

What struck me most was the lack of sophistication, from a business perspective, that most plant-touching cannabis entrepreneurs had. In retrospect, it is easy to understand why this is the case. The majority of these folks had been working in the shadows for the duration of their career and did not have access or exposure to many of the systems, norms, even acronyms that folks with my background had. From zero to one was the level that many of the original advocates of the industry felt they could achieve. With new talent, the question wasn't how long it would take to get to one, but how long it would take to get to the first million.

Mirroring my own journey, the industry began to seek its own highest common denominator – transforming illicit market misconceptions into education and reform; shifting public thought from dangerous drug to medicine. Much like my own syntax emerged as a product of my desire, the syntax of the industry has shifted.

Consume instead of smoke.

Consumer instead of stoner.

Cannabis instead of pot.

The optics were altered.

Storefronts of dispensaries were minimalist.

Methods of consumption were altered.

The individuals in the industry began to break through the stoner stereotype.

Cannabis is just one part of my story. I was an employee, an entrepreneur, an alumni of a top tier university where I worked at excelling at programming and visual design, and most of all, a student of life.

In the world of cannabis, I found that there was a myriad of people looking to rise – elevated and advanced - using the industry as a vector to harnessing success.

My journey continues to be a function of value sets. I'm not interested in distilling myself down to numbers, nor do I believe that statistics, stereotypes, or tropes determine mine or anyone's worth. I'm looking to connect at a level that is continuously rising, finding a joint mission irrespective of any variable except the ones of drive, vision, and humility.

I'm looking to go higher.

Open the Loop of Passion

passion

|passion|

noun

an intense desire or enthusiasm for something

Find your ikigai, and you will find your passion. Have you heard this before? Ikigai is a fundamental Japanese concept that essentially boils down to this: find your reason for waking up in the morning; find your reason for being.

Ikigai is one word that is made up of two parts--"iki," which means life and "gai" which means value or worth. Together these words mean "the value of doing and the value of working," and to some, the word itself may even represent happiness. But, ikigai is not to be confused with happiness. Happiness, as we will discuss later, is a state of being that is defined by your own desire. Your ikigai is more like a roadmap to your future, a guiding principle; happiness may be the outcome of finding your ikigai (depending on how you define it).

Living a fulfilling life is a matter of finding your passion, following it, and intersecting it with reality. And how do you do this? You find the balance that exists among a series of intersections:

- What you love vs. what the world needs

- What you love vs. what you can be paid for
- What you love vs. what you are good at

This balance can be hard to find, primarily when what fulfills you does not offer you a way to fill your bank account. So, how do you find this? Well first, you must find out what you are passionate about and then you need to find the medium through which you can express that passion. For example, if your college major was Medieval Studies and you do not want to get your Ph.D. or go on to be a professor, you can think outside of the box of standard careers and think about where your skills might be needed. This can be challenging, especially because you must think outside of the box of societal expectations and constrictions. So, why not start a career as a consultant for filmmakers seeking to produce films on this time period? You could intersect with your passion every day and make a pretty penny while you do so. For most of us, this is not something that we think of because we are so conditioned to follow the status quo, but you can transcend that baseline and still find a balance.

My passion is finding opportunity. By my profession, I am a technologist and an entrepreneur. I am good at coding, leading, and being a champion of culture. Each of those things fits into the job that I carried out at Baker. I found success in my work at Baker, and this, in turn, allowed for me to find even more opportunity, which I am passionate about. By my nature, I am a technologist, and I am good at it. I am also good at the things I described above, each of which allowed me to perform my role better. I felt fulfilled by the way that I intersected with what I wanted and what I needed/what the world needed.

It may seem daunting to start filling in the gaps that define your ikigai, especially if you cannot quite identify either what your passion is or how to fit it into your life and still be successful. As you go through this journey, ask yourself these questions:

1. What interests me? (Food, technology, science?)

2. What sort of lifestyle do I want to live? (Do you want to live in the hills of Malibu or drive across the country in a van?)

3. What access do you have? (Who comprises your current tribe? How can you find ways to leverage more access?)

4. How much effort are you willing to put in to get access to what you do not already have access to? (How much are you ready to sacrifice?)

5. What sort of impact on society is more important to you? (Do you want to help others?)

6. What is the effect that you want for yourself? (Do you want your work to make you famous? Or would you instead operate in the shadows?)

Then, you need to look at your circumstances and ask yourself a subset of questions such as these:

1.   How does my culture fit in my passion and my goals?

2.   Could my race or socioeconomic status affect my access as I try to achieve my goals?

When you answer these questions, be real with yourself. Don't just tell yourself what you want to hear or what you think society wants you to say. Your ikigai is true to you, and to find it; you have to break down the walls that have prevented you from seeing it in the first place. This is your chance to be entirely and fully honest with the highest and most integral parts of yourself. You owe this integrity to yourself and your growth.

Passion is linear. The way that we intersect our passion with practically is not. It is dynamic and requires research, introspection, and interactions. Really, if you think about it, your loop of passion is not just your ikigai, it is the highest common denominator. It is a culmination of intersections at the highest level of thought that get you to exactly where you want to go.

Now, here is the exciting part – while I have identified my ikigai and I know how to intersect at the HCD, I have no idea what is next for me. I do not know

where life will take me next but what I do know is this – if I
continue to intersect at the highest common denominator,
I will end up in a place that fits my ikigai.

HIGH FIVE
by DAVID TRAN

David Tran is the founder of Dope Magazine, one of the most impactful publications in cannabis. His insight is the culmination of twenty years of immersion in leading the cannabis narrative to advocate for wellness, empowerment, and diversity for all.

High five. A greeting of inclusion, of empowerment, of acknowledgment of the difficulty of sometimes fitting in. Venturing out, even venturing in, these aren't easy endeavors. I see these people, standing on the edge of greatness, and I want to put my arm around their shoulders, and walk them into this room, this conversation, this world. A high-five is the way that I can show my encouragement to those that are considering their path - onwards, and upwards. I want everyone to connect on a higher plane, where opportunity is abundant and acceptance into the community, and also of yourself, is the goal.

I didn't have a lot of people who looked like me, growing up in Seattle. In my neighborhood and my church - wherever I went, I was the outsider. The outside didn't matter. My mom was a Vietnamese refugee who worked nonstop - typical immigrant story, I know - but raising five kids in the ghetto wasn't easy for her, and it isn't easy for anyone. I didn't know where I fit in - too ethnic for the white kids and too white-washed for my community. On the inside, even, I wasn't black and white, black or white. I was trying to be the good student, but I was the spiffy dresser, and in some ways, the perfect son. I helped my grandfather, (as only a little and lazy kid could, by hammering a nail or just keeping him company) a visionary and selfless man, build the first Vietnamese church in Seattle, board by board and brick by brick. I lived in service of making those around me proud but didn't feel a fire burning in my heart. I walked the path but didn't pave my own.

I didn't fit in, and so I didn't stand out.

I loved my community, but something just always felt like it could go in a different direction. I felt like I was being pulled, away from the black and white world of social norms and acceptance.

The day that I lit my first joint however, I was engulfed. I suddenly felt a sense of calm wash over me, this plant flowing through my body and extinguishing some deep-seated pains. Every inhale was like a breath of fresh air. I started to immerse myself in the counterculture of cannabis in the early 90's - the iconic stewards who grew the plant, and the industry. More than that, they cultivated a culture of inclusion and community - for the first time, I belonged somewhere. I wasn't too much of this or too little of that - I was just me.

In cannabis, color didn't matter.

Even my clothes had a transformation, and my mom, a strict and devout Catholic, noticed. Instead of excluding this evolved version of myself, she brought me closer, accepting the man I chose to be. College became a breeding ground of joining others who preserved the cannabis culture decades ago - we weren't just the stoners who smoked to get high (although hell yeah we did), we were people who learned how to grow and nourish a plant, and by doing so, support and encourage each other. Being a minority in the outside world was a barrier, but in the world of cannabis, it didn't even play a part. We were all minorities in this space - under-represented, under-served, and stereotyped. Stoners, criminals, lazy. Whatever the title, we didn't shy away, because the power of our tribe was so much more of an identity than any arbitrary title that society ignorantly gave us.

I witnessed, firsthand, the negativity and stigma of being involved in cannabis - similar, in fact, to being a person of color, a woman, or even from a "bad" neighborhood. Not only was the ignorance of society affecting our ability to grow the plant and the industry, but it was also deeply affecting the ability of medical patients to gain access.

There were hoops on top of hoops, and intelligent minds were discouraged from lending their talents to supporting access or creating a positive conversation around its benefits.

I couldn't sit idly by - it isn't who I am. So, I started to stand up - for people, for the plant, for the philosophy of what cannabis is, what it can do, and why we need it in our society.

DOPE Magazine was born out of this mindset - Defending Our Patients Everywhere was the core mission of our words - we told stories, encouraged education, and presented the plant for the world to see - no lies, no gimmicks, no agenda. Just an exposure that illuminated the truth, and our audience grew, as the industry moved to the light.

We featured innovators and users, growers and consumers. We shared tips, stories, and brands. We narrated the world of cannabis to curious minds, and as the push towards legalization spread across the United States, we leveraged our words.

This is where I met Roger - when words became action. His logic was new to me - simple, honest, and passionate. To connect on the level of a shared mission spoke volumes to me and our mission at DOPE, which, after years of being a voice for patients, is now a voice for the plant. Roger and I shared a philosophy of inclusion.

As he brought people in, from diverse backgrounds of life and careers, the voices in our industry expanded and grew. He mentored minds to understand the value of the industry and the value of creating elevated products. He wasn't afraid to speak out, and so people listened.

So did I.

Some people say that cannabis has evolved. I think our world has evolved. The plant has always, and will always be a powerful tool to connect and encourage our health, both mental and physical.

It needed stewards to guide its journey from the darkness to light. It needed voices to give it a voice. Like so many waiting on the edge of greatness, it needed a high-five from a world ready to accept its power.

To greet new minds at the door, I think we should put our arms around each other, and walk into the future together.

It all starts with a high-five.

CHAPTER 2

WHAT IS A TRIBE?

Finding and forming a tribe is a function of learning what you want, and who you are. Living outside of the comfort zone that society has set can be a risky endeavor, because to challenge the status quo, you have to break social norms. To me, that challenge was an inspiration that kept the question alive: why is my potential constricted? Whom am I serving by staying stagnant? The urgency to change can be challenging, and I could not wait to realize my potential. I exposed myself because it was my only chance to understand what the world had to offer, and what I had to offer it.

So, I followed my passion and found my potential. In finding cannabis, I didn't just see the green - I saw the reality. I could not pretend that the adverse drug policies, philosophies, and the perverse criminal policies that disproportionately destroyed people didn't exist.

They did, and do.

But, where there is ruin, there is hope for treasure.

I love cannabis, and when Baker was born, I had to make a decision to instill the ethos into the community that was the differentiator between survival of the tribe, and its thriving potential.

***

I am good at a few things: analyzing, programming, and networking. I can be paid for being a developer, consultant, and hell, maybe even a web designer. I am passionate about art, cooking, and creating. The world can use my skills: can't it?

The impetus, the goal, the origin of my desire, or need, or capability—whatever you want to call it—to grow beyond the borders of the expectations placed upon me, were simple: I had to. The urge to create outside the lines of opportunities "granted" to me was so strong, that I often chose the path that had a statistically large failure rate. I pursued the path of creating, innovating, and exploring my opportunities because I wanted to create the one thing that so few of us have—the one great equalizer—optionality.

I had to reconcile my abilities, my desires, my opportunities (and how viable they were), and most critically, their value, and mine, to the world.

To enter the world of options, I first needed an exit.

And that is where we start.

At the beginning of my exit.

People often ask me how they can do what I did, referring to the success my partners and I had with the conception, and then ultimately, the exit from our company, Baker Technologies.

I am more than willing to answer the question, but

I don't always know how to respond without sounding dismissive, or even to some, abrasive. The very minute that I hear those words leave someone's mouth, I make an internal judgment. You can't, I think. This initial thought has nothing to do with the individual's capabilities. It has to do with his or her circumstances. So, instead of giving a two-word response, I sift through potential responses in my mind, trying to live up to the expectations of the optimistic person standing before me. I could be frank and say option A is sleep in your intern's closet and find a way to survive on barely a 1/10 of what you could make someplace else. My co-founders and I agreed that to put our company's potential first, our personal needs (alternative opportunities) would have to come last. Instead of pursuing careers with secure paychecks, we chose the risky route of uncertainty for the same reason that so many do: our vision outstripped our comfort. For many entrepreneurs, the mentality of comfort just feels uncomfortable. The sacrifice seems worth the potential upside. And maybe that is all potential is: infinite options that could materialize versus a finite reality.

Option B is to sell your house and hope for the best (which can be difficult when your family depends on you to sustain a certain livable basic income).

I could, however, be blunt (one of my trademark characteristics) and let them know the internal conclusion of my quick inventory: "You can't. The conditions of your circumstance are not primed for this type of marathon." For the vast majority of us, endless capital isn't in the cards, and so these A/B options are our only choice in the pursuit of creation. Ships, it is said, are safe in harbor. Like ships, we are built for more than safety. Open waters mean experiences that become lessons, lessons that become tools, tools that become keys to unlock choices.

As I said, I was hungry for choices, and risked my career safety to go higher. I chose to try.

So, when I stand in front of hopeful entrepreneurs, recently validated on the market as a "successful founder with a successful exit from a company," I don't mean to squash their dreams with a dose of jaded reality. I just mean it practically; many people cannot do what I did the way that I did it because they have a family or a mortgage and most probably, cannot bear to sacrifice losing those things.

So, I hesitate—rapidly recollecting on the life that led me here: do I tell them about the closet I slept in, in a two-bedroom apartment in Colorado with two other guys? Do I tell them about how I sacrificed decent meals despite the fact that I revere food with the same passion that New Yorkers treasure the Yankees? Do I tell them about the twenty years spent consulting and in start-ups waiting for this moment? Do I tell them that a lot of people aren't willing to sacrifice what I did to get where I am?

There is no secret recipe for what I accomplished. That fact of the matter is that my success was a combination of hard work, self-awareness, pragmatism, careful curation, and sheer determination. I fell, failed, and restarted many times.

Every crack of failure is a chance to recreate a stronger bond. I found that through studying the perspectives of others, I was able to fortify my toolbox of growth more efficiently, as wisdom comes in so many ways.

I have always resonated with the Japanese culture. One of my favorite Japanese proverbs—"Fall down seven, stand up eight"—states that failure is a part of success. Success, I was taught, teaches us nothing. It takes failure to learn, and I am a student of life.

Sometimes, you might question your entire journey when you lose certain battles. But what choice do you have, if not to stand up to the inevitable odds? Doing this takes an indescribable hunger to accomplish your goals— but there is no supplement to that appetite. Either you are committed to it, or you are not.

Now, some traits, ambition for example, aren't always inherent, but with the right mind-set, they can be learned, implemented, and executed. We can breed the necessary traits.

When I try to explain to people how I became

successful, I rely on the granular details that define my success—facets of my life that upon introspection, were the reason I met my goals. I will expand on this later in our conversation.

I've pondered on what led me to this point and learned that to create a more equitable and empowering future, I needed to dissect my past—the moments and decisions from my beginning that came to shape my future. Why? Because in order to get where I wanted, I had to come to terms with where I came from. I needed to understand it and own it so that I could leverage it, not use it as my cross to bear.

Primal urges for assimilation cannot be ignored, but they do not need to define our decisions. Our primal nature must be acknowledged and understood so that we can move past it. Our ancestors required assimilation for survival. In most circumstances, we do not need to assimilate to survive, yet the desire is burned into our DNA. If we understand this, we will be better equipped to separate from the herd, or as Thoreau might say, "live in the woods."

These words make it sound easy, like separating from everything that you know is a casual stroll down the street. It is not easy. Breaking from your herd means you break down walls, walls that exist not just in society but in our very genetic makeup. We are supposed to stay shackled to our herd. We are not supposed to differentiate ourselves, because standing out becomes a matter of survival.

Sometimes the echo chamber feels good, we feel validated by what we know and less alienated by the world around us. Yet, this chamber exists as a comfort, as a light for those who fear the dark. The real growth comes when you gain multiple perspectives from a bird's-eye view. But this often requires being willing to walk through an unknown territory without a flashlight.

Leaving what you know also means questioning its value in the first place. An objective, not subjective perspective, is critical for our evolution beyond the borders of an identity prescribed by the tribe. Without the facts, we are clouded by emotion-filled thoughts that serve no purpose but to tether us to our tribe. If we can't look at ourselves or our tribe objectively, we stop short of growth. Ignorance won't lead us anywhere.

Know Your Tribe and Stray from It
tribe
/trīb/
noun

a social division in a traditional society consisting of families or communities linked by social, economic, religious, or blood ties, with a common culture and dialect

I'm the typical American. Actually, I think I'm the typical American—I was born in a small suburb in New Jersey, my parents were working-class Costa Rican immigrants, our house had a mortgage, and our Friday evenings were spent watching TGIF on ABC while eating dinner. The only thing missing from this picture-perfect American life was the dog, which much to my dismay was adopted after I left for college. I'm still bitter.

From the perspective of my peers in my very Italian neighborhood, even, I was pretty normal. I don't look like Americans' idea of "Hispanic." I reserved my Spanish speaking for my yearly summer trips to Costa Rica, I ate Italian heroes for lunch, and most of all, I just didn't feel that I was any different from any of my classmates. It was all the Italians, and me. In that way, we had already expanded the definition of our tribe. We all felt as uniquely American as anyone else.

It's true that at home I may have grown up on rice and beans, chicharrones, and tortillas, but make no mistake, I was as American as a Kennedy. I grew up cheering for the Mets and the Giants. I played basketball at the park across the street from my house from sunrise to sunset on weekends. I was listening to A Tribe Called Quest's Low End Theory on repeat in the autumn of 1991. I would hang out with friends at the mall with no money, but at least we tasted the freedom of an unsupervised afternoon.

OK, so maybe a Kennedy isn't the best comparison, but I grew up as American as apple pie nonetheless.

Because of that perception, I didn't tend to align with the narrative, customs, or religious ties that were the binders of my heritage. In fact, my father, a skilled woodworker, had made a conscientious decision to shed his own "Costa-Rican-ness" when he immigrated—he lost his accent, he made American friends, and most of all, he expanded his scope of social interactions. This conscious effort that my father made to immerse us into unfamiliar surroundings was critical in creating a new identity.

For all intents and purposes, we were Americans.

But in many ways, the title felt ambiguous.

"Ethnically Ambiguous" is a term that has often been used to describe me. Looking at myself in the mirror it is easy to understand why. I am tall, olive skinned, have dark hair, wear thick-rimmed eyeglasses, and my arms are covered in Japanese tattoos. I look like either a hipster or a nerd, and so the world tends to stare quizzically, trying to find the bucket to which I belong, but the problem is, I don't seem to fit a pattern. I too, would guess at my ethnicity. But anonymity, like ambiguity, has its perks. Until recently I hadn't realized how much that ambivalence was benefitting me.

If the world was curious, I was sure.

Growing up I was well aware of the fact that I was a

first-generation Costa Rican.

That didn't really mean much back then because the only other Costa Ricans I knew were my aunt, uncle, and cousin who lived an hour away. I actually lived in a Sicilian neighborhood in "mob country"—take from that what you will. We did not have a community to get lost in, like many other people of Latin American descent despite the large community of Costa Ricans living in New Jersey.

Despite that, the robust diverse community of Hispanics, Italians, and the sporadic inclusion of African Americans that existed in my hometown was constantly seeking to immerse kids into their cultural and social philosophies—pride of heritage, of country of origin, and perhaps most critical (and in my opinion, most damaging), an expectation of society based purely on the brownness or lack thereof of our shared continental heritage. These arbitrary shared traits have no real basis in reality—a human being's individual traits are not culturally appropriated or even homogenous. They are the results of our personal experiences reconciled with our personal incentives to learn, or not. We aren't all learning at the same pace, and can't. Lumping our shared heritage with our individual experience is an ignorant way to align. More so, assuming that our shared baseline traits somehow align us on a higher plane is just lazy and honestly, archaic. The world is advancing and connecting. So too, should we.

To entirely ignore the value of our shared roots, however, is as equally ignorant in making them the sole impetus of our existence. There is safety in numbers—hence the tribe—so it is a natural mechanism of social order. Venturing outside that herd mentality is hard—people are both marble and sculptor in the creation of themselves—and so forging individuals is a challenge, often unsupported by society. We also have to think of our parents in respecting the sacrifices so many have made in creating a new life in a new land. Ignoring our history seems a slap in the face to them, so we toe the line of the old culture despite our new one.

The echo chamber of being forced to remain aligned with your birth tribe also closes the door to diversity of experience and thought, and so anyone who looks different, just feels foreign.

We aren't taught to speak the same language of connectivity, and because of that, so many of our shared human experiences are just lost in translation.

This lack of a desire to understand people unlike yourself, this "us versus them" mentality, the concept of "different" being less than—these facets of cultural identity just never sat well with my curiosity.

But that claim also didn't align with my personal experiences—in the United States I was Hispanic, a couple of shades away from an American. In Costa Rica, I was an American, a few shades away from a true Costa Rican.

As I said, I was "ethnically ambiguous." I never fit into a group—not just because of my heritage but because I never wanted to be a part of just one group. I wanted to build a modular Roger—taking parts of one mentality, segments of another, and creating an optimized version that experienced cultures, ideas, and the world with an open mind. I didn't want to be told who I was. I wanted to figure it out for myself.

In school, I was a good student—driven, responsible, and interested. I earned my way into honors programs as a function of my hard work and merit. Despite the meritocracy of my grades, I was in many ways just another kid from an underserved town. The outside world viewed us as hardly unique no matter our efforts, because South Hackensack was just South Hackensack. We were aligned by our lowest traits—little opportunity from a little town.

I was underprivileged and underserved, yet the powers that be decided that my group was in dire need of assistance to achieve an arbitrary set of goals that were deemed achievable. The caveat of this, of course, was that these goals were determined to be the height of what we were considered capable of achieving, not what we could actually achieve. Even our dreams were given ceilings.

We were told to dream within the confines of our realities and not the vastness of imagination. These limited dreams we were given were born from a set of beliefs based on propaganda, social class, and a top-down system. These programs did not prepare us for a potential life; they prepared us to live within the bounds of societal expectation. We were first labeled, then limited, then prepped to live within the lines.

Social equity programs are not the problem. They are an attempt at a solution to an engineered social reality: institutions create borders, borders dictated by our most baseline traits. We are grouped in the laziest of ways: color, creed, or gender.

The mentality of connecting us based on these baselines, typically from stakeholders who succeed if we fail, try to harness and dictate our ambition, brainwashing us into thinking that the broken dreams of a corrupt system are our own. At a young age, where imagination should exist infinitely within the confines of our tangible minds, is in reality, finite. Our value is predetermined by our label, and so too is our self-worth.

Had I not desired a life without limits, I would be living within the confines of what was expected of me. I had a few routes that were preplanned, but beyond those borders, I was directionless.

I had to forge my own path, leveraging the dull tools given to me. Either way, I sharpened my focus and started to build.

I have always resolved to work hard, and through that, I earned my ticket to a life outside of the one I had been living. To get where I wanted to go, I had no choice but to take advantage of what was offered to me—minority inclusion programs, secondary education, and any number of mentors. Don't get me wrong—I never just took what was given to me. I did not want to remain static, so I analyzed and evaluated exactly what I could leverage to gain an advantage. The baseline was my starting point (as it was for most others), but I was certain that it would not be my endpoint. Much like building Legos, I took pieces that were intended to become, let's say, buildings, and retrofit them into (I'm reaching, but making a point—stick with me), spaceships. The point is, I took what I was given, looked at it creatively, and then tried to finagle it into something else.

Spaceships are a product of thousands (millions?) of pieces compiled by hundreds (thousands?) of people. All of the different parts—bolts, panels, signage—no matter how seemingly inconsequential they appear, are the sum total of a joint endeavor in which every step is iterative and imperative. The process of creating yourself is no different—every moment, every interaction, every lesson can be evaluated and leveraged to benefit your evolution.

Yet, I was frustrated. Frustrated that I had to enroll in inclusion programs while other people (privileged kids with legacy families and parents in big business) could simply just step through the door. Even though my world didn't operate with the same rules, I was well aware that it could.

Before I could do anything, I had to face the stark reality that my tribe was not likely to help me get where I wanted to go. Oftentimes this is hard—we identify with our tribe; their blood runs through us. Yet, sometimes in order to align with our own ideals, we have to break away (unless we want to be limited by our circumstances). If I had succumbed to my circumstances, I might have subscribed to the life that so many of my tribesmen chose—working five miles from where I was born in a family business. Don't get me wrong—if this is what you want, go for it! What drove them, however, never drove me. I felt unsettled by settling for what I was told I should do versus what I knew I wanted to do. Maybe it was my glasses, but I saw success through a different lens. I saw the potential that life had to offer, if I only looked beyond the borders.

With this realization I had to begin to differentiate between what was probable and what was possible. It was probable that I would work five miles from where I grew up, but I also saw the potential to live a life different from the one that was laid out for me.

In my family, college was hoped for, but not

required. At home, the bar wasn't set for success based singularly on education, but a holistic view of happiness and contentment. My parents wanted me to work hard and iterate on the life that they gave me. Happiness and health were their highest hopes for my life, and pushing from a place of love was their philosophy. There was an expectation, but not a pressure. My parents did not go to college and because of this they had no context for it—it was a binary thing for them. Go or don't go.

College was never binary for me—there was no possibility in my mind that my journey would not include higher education. I knew that I wanted to go, but the only question I asked myself was, "Which one do I really want to attend, and more importantly, why?" I knew that I needed to attend college in order to increase my access to opportunities in life—the great equalizer is the same competitive starting point. So, I gave them a talking-to, explaining the 'whys' and 'hows' of my decision to pursue the path of an expensive, faraway, and elevated education. They had respect for my perspective and listened to everything that I had to say about it. I may have had to explain myself more than the typical high-schooler, but they were all ears when I explained that despite the fact that I had a full ride at Rutgers, I would be better served by attending Duke. In a lot of ways, their openness to my choices (college decisions included) helped to make me who I am today. They had a willingness to hear what I had to say, and they trusted that I knew what I was talking about. My life, until that point, had proven that.

Given what I told you, you can likely assume that it was not probable that I would attend college. Why? College was not an expectation in my social circle or community. I did not have parents who went to Stanford and USC, as others with whom I was competing did, and as a result they had a different context for their lives. College was probable for them. If anyone from my circle wanted to attend college, they had to earn their way there. Where we lived dictated what we had access to. Since we had less access than the more privileged sectors of society we had to jump through more hoops, we had to create our own scaffolds, and curate our own support groups. The system is designed to keep us down, so we had to do more in order to rise.

People around me did not know how to dress the part or speak it for that matter. The education was average; I had to take advantage of every bit of information that I could in my public-school classroom. Public-school education, by the way, can be an incredible resource if leveraged correctly, but the conditions in which many learn are often standardized, and not optimized. The amount of information that pertained to gaining access to college was limited, and if available, so complex that many probably simply shied away.

The pressure to gather the facts then, fell squarely on my own shoulders, but I honestly felt compelled to conduct it—there was no other way to advance myself without access to the seemingly vast resources and networks that college afforded. My research was, for all intents and purposes, self-propagated and self-motivated. In the beginning, I had no idea what a "good" school was—there was no context for that. I educated myself to educate myself. I learned the art of perception—that which is considered better, ultimately becomes a benchmark. The difficulty was applying my logic to those echelons and trying to understand, and maybe even ultimately revere, those perceptions as well. Every day of my learning revealed another component of this process, and the more I learned, the less complicated it seemed. By breaking the goal into steps, and climbing each step with preparation and insight, I realized that it was easy to step higher if I could incrementally move up.

There was so much noise that surrounded this learning experience, that I had to learn how to tune out the white-and-black nature of it all. "This" college, I was told, was right for minorities; "that" college, they said, was perfect for athletes; but "the" college that I wanted to attend wasn't for someone like me.

I tuned it out—to stay on course, only my desire

mattered. I wanted a university experience that met my criteria—strong academic leadership, an immersive experience, distance from my home life (a trap of comfort), an elevated prestige, and as a result, a network of accomplished minds.

I chose and went to Duke without visiting once—it was purely empirical. Tangentially, it is not a school that is just about academics. It is a school known for its basketball program, which I equated to "culture," even though if pressed, I wouldn't have been able to verbalize it at the time. What I knew, however, was that it appealed to me on many levels, and I wanted to be multifaceted. Being multifaceted is equitable to more opportunity. The more you know, the more you can do. I wanted to do more.

Maybe as you read this you are thinking: I did not come from the same background that you did. My family had money. I went to a great school. I had access to opportunity. Why do I need to go beyond my tribe?

You need to for the same reason that I did—to enhance your worldview and familiarize yourself with the unknown. We all have room to grow. You can't expect change if you won't. You can't get anywhere by staying where you are.

Reaching into your discomfort zone—outside of your comfort zone isn't about shedding what works—it is about optimizing it.

For example, I advanced my access to opportunity because I used my circumstance as a vector instead of a crutch. I felt conflicted over this at times—I did not want to seem like I was wading in the ocean holding up my immigrant card so that someone would come and save me. But, I had to acknowledge that my status set the odds against me. Once I did, I was able to level my concerns with logic—my status became a tool. I had to weigh the benefits of what was offered to me as a result of my circumstance while reconciling my alignment with a merit-based existence. Turns out being Hispanic helps not just with college admissions but with grants and scholarships. It was hard not to grab at the low-hanging fruit of opportunity that financial assistance allowed, and I felt, and feel, no shame in this. I catalyzed myself by utilizing the tools available to me, not abusing them. The misconceptions that surround these programs are that the recipient is entirely undeserving of the rewards. For the majority of hardworking students, that is categorically untrue. We don't begin at the same point on the starting line—in fact, we aren't even sure we will get a ride to the race. We run our asses off to even have a chance at competing, and then the race starts. These programs take those hurdles into account, and provide at least the running shoes required to finish the race. My wife, Andrea, really said it best: "Social equality isn't about giving opportunity away; it is about providing opportunity for all."

The truth was, I needed the help if I did not want to come out with the overly excessive burden of student loans. I had to face the fact that yes, I was Hispanic, but I was also a hard worker and a high achiever. In fact, I probably had to work harder than most of the other applicants. Idealistic struggles aside, I made the choice that was best for me and went on a path that my tribe did not forge.

As I ventured outside the ideals of my tribe, I kept pieces of my heritage and my upbringing close to me, but I never let them define me. They were a part of me, but they were not me. Don't get me wrong, I was not trying to deny my heritage nor would I ever. Instead, I was trying to elevate what it meant for that to be a part of me. If I went to a top-tier college and found extreme success in big business so too could another one of my tribe. As a result of my hope and my drive, I was able to deny what was expected of me and transform my world.

Where was the meritocracy—the system designed to earn your way based on metrics, on efforts, and on alignment with peers who mirrored your goals? I will tell you where it was—it did not exist outside of the idealized definition of our world. How could it exist in a world where the rich have opportunities that the poor do not? In a world where money reigns king, it only makes sense that the rich would be privy to the privilege of "easy" opportunity. If you don't have the money, you don't have the immediate opportunity (unless of course you work for it). That is just the way of our world.

I was never just given anything. My dad did not work in big business. He did not have connections who could get me an internship or a place in a fancy private school. My family did not have a legacy at an Ivy League school. I had to work for what I wanted, and I ended up earning my way to the top because of that. While the system may have frustrated me, hard work was never something that I strayed from.

Some people say I am honest to a fault. I would have to disagree—there is no fault in honesty. To me, honesty is a matter of honor, it is a genuine and transparent aspect of moral character. I align with this authenticity because I believe that things are what they seem, and there is no need to make them into more than what they must be. That said, I will say this. I love my family, but I look beyond my tribe. I disliked how it defined me before I could even begin to define myself. This statement is not an easy one to make. It can be hard to admit that your family or your community is not in line with your ideals. But you must be honest with yourself. If you do not align, alter your circumstance and steer your ship in another direction.

I can't recall when I decided to leave my tribe, but I knew I couldn't live in the box of a single identity forever.

Intermingling became the tool to expand my worldview. The idea of spending my entire life in the same place and knowing only what I was taught to know seemed suffocating. From a small neighborhood to major cities across the world, I was intent on immersing, growing, and challenging my comfort level. Outside the bounds of your safety, lies opportunity.

So, if you are in a position or a place that you do not like, change it. The world is already in motion—it is up to you to get your own life started. So, set yourself in motion, find your balance amid the instability, and create a life that aligns with your passions.

I know what you are thinking. "Well, Roger— Mr. Practical—it is not always that easy to just 'change it.'" What I want you to know is, it is that easy, we just overcomplicate it with emotions. We subconsciously manufacture hurdles to our own success. As though it is not hard enough just to be human, we make it harder. We let anxieties and fears get in the way of our chance to change. At the intersection of fear and desire we fall into the cliché of becoming our own worst enemies. Together, the polar opposites—fear and desire—become barriers to our ability to make a choice. All too often we indulge our own vulnerabilities, destroying our own chance for change with none other than self-inflicted doubt.

Identifying, understanding, and then facing fears is

the only way to conquer them, not avoid them.

There is nothing easy about the choice to change things—it is long, arduous, and unforgiving. But removing the complications means unfastening the mental barriers that keep us both comforted, and uncomfortable at the same time. And the only way to break the barriers is to forge through them like you are ripping off a Band-Aid. You need to learn to do this so that you can stop throwing away opportunities (which come around only every so often).

The point is, although you might feel hopeful of achieving your dreams, but scared to sacrifice, you will only make a choice when one or the other—complacency versus discontent—no longer serves you. When the choice to leave overpowers your will to stay, life will change.

You can change your life but you must be willing to hold hands with sacrifice (which is difficult in a world where we are expected to live large, or in many cases, remain stagnant). The temptation of living an "easier life" may seem alluring but is your "easier life" making you happy? Is this the path that your younger self would have chosen? If it is not, change it. The journey might include ramen noodles or a move to a new city, but the path is always worth it. My point is this: If you follow your desire and make the required sacrifices, then what you give up can come back to you tenfold.

Life, then, is a matter of perspective. We make things harder than they have to be. At the end of the day, you are the captain of your ship. Only you can steer it.

In my world, life happens once. Chances are just that—chances. They aren't guarantees, and you can't bank on a redo. The only way forward is to design a life of your choice, here, and now. I am not challenging your beliefs on life; I am challenging you to live one that makes you happy.

Ignorance Is Not Bliss

ignorance

/ignorance/

noun

lack of knowledge or information

Face it—to do more, you need to know more—and while the web is an almost infinite resource, there is no replacement for the real thing: full immersion into an experience different than the one that you already know.

As a boy, I spent my summers in Costa Rica—these adventures gave me a taste of a world that was totally opposite to my daily life.

The moment after the last bell rang, signaling the end of the school year, I would be whisked away to see my extended family in Costa Rica. This "whisking" was the result of months of penny-pinching, saving, and meticulous planning to afford our time away. It was imperative to my parents that we did not lose the connection to their families, and their history.

It always seemed like an exotic otherworldly place to me. I was painfully aware that there, I was the alien. It was not home, but it was not foreign. Whenever we got to Costa Rica my parents embraced it, plunging back into the world where they came from. I tried to do the same, looking at it as an opportunity to sharpen my Spanish— which I always did by each summer's end.

I volleyed between English thoughts and Spanish words, to Spanish thoughts and ideas. In the early weeks of the summer, I would oftentimes get stuck on Spanish words; as the weeks turned into months, the language began to flow. I would weave in colloquialisms as the locals did and as I did this, I felt a sense of pride. And then nine months later, after many months back in the States, bits and pieces of the native mannerisms I had worked so hard to understand stayed in my brain but not on my tongue. The duality of my heritage and the subtle translations from mouth to mind came to represent the subconscious battle I so often had. I was Hispanic. I was American. I was never ignorant to either one. Yet, I was so much more than both of them. You too are so much more than the label of your heritage. My success was a function of my tenacity. However, my enhanced understanding of the world that complemented my success was a result of the many worlds I lived in and saw.

These summers redefined not just my notion of being poor but highlighted how different my expectations of life were. Had I never seen the trenches of Costa Rica, I would not have known what true simplicity looked like or just how lucky I was to live the life that I did back in New Jersey.

Prior to these experiences, I was ignorant to what my own life was truly like. Interestingly enough, my family in Costa Rica was as ignorant to what I had back at home as I was to what they had; at least in the beginning. I had what they did not know that they needed. Eventually the ignorant qualms became one sided—instead of trying to understand where I came from, my family made judgments. I never wanted to be like this. I never wanted judgment to take the place of true understanding. I wanted to fill in the blanks because I had the understanding and knowledge to do so. To me, there is nothing attractive about ignorance. Ignorance is lazy; it is inhibiting. Had I ever allowed myself to be ignorant to any of my situations, I never would have gained from the experience. To be truly fulfilled by an experience, you must keep an open mind. This was something that I did even at a young age. For example, life in Costa Rica was different (as I mentioned), and I was faced with experiences that were not considered part of the norm.

Much like my perceptions of the world around me, they were contextualized.

On these journeys to my homeland, I had to throw context out the window, because when I talk about these circumstances in Costa Rica two things stand out to me—cockroaches and cold showers.

Cockroaches were the norm in my grandmother's home in Costa Rica. They were not a topic of concerned discussion—the doors were always left open, and the roaches were free to roam indoors. They might as well have made a tiny bed for these pests with how easily they accepted their presence. As you know, cockroaches in the United States are associated with filth and poverty. A cockroach in the hallway of a home in the United States could warrant a frantic conversation and an immediate call to pest control. Judgments would abound. Gross. Dirty. Yuck, people would think. Had I grown up in Costa Rica, I would never have known cockroaches to be anything other than irritating pests, but not a reflection of our cleanliness.

Speaking of random visitors, hot water should not be in that category—it should be a constant companion. In my grandmother's home, if you wanted hot water in your shower, you would have to turn the switch on the electrical showerhead. The catch? The shower head was plugged into the wall as you stood in a puddle of water below the spout. It was like you were standing in a chamber designed for your electrocution. It was not uncommon to get shocked while you fiddled with them. I remember standing there, my feet tethered to the rubber mat, wishing so badly that I was back in New Jersey. Luckily, electrocution was not as common as one would think, and the mild shocks were more frightening than they were damaging. I always felt lucky that these were not conditions I had to deal with back home. At the time I did not feel as grateful for what I had back at home as I should have; in retrospect, having access to an expanded worldview was instrumental in who I became.

These summers gave me a frame of reference that helped me to categorize what I wanted my success to be. From these trips I was able to form a more well-rounded picture of society, allowing me to better contextualize my world.

I never wanted to have a myopic perspective of anything.

I tell you this to remind you to take advantage of those opportunities that enhance your perspective. If opportunity knocks, answer it. Learn everything you can, and add each experience into your toolbox. You never know when you will need to use one of your tools as a resource. I can promise you that when the time comes to use it, you will be grateful that you have it.

In a lot of ways, my need to have a worldly perspective shaped the desire I had to add diversity to Baker. I knew from my own experience just how important it was to bring in people from different backgrounds. For a majority of my career experience, you could throw a dart in any given room and be sure to hit a privileged man. Don't get me wrong here; I have worked with a lot of exceptional people who came from privileged backgrounds, but I had also come to understand the heights to which we can rise if we are knowledgeable about diversity. We can do so much if we do it together—if we do it with people of different skin colors, genders, ethnicities, and sexual orientations.

We should not hide beneath the cliché of "ignorance is bliss." It is not bliss; it is impractical and uninformed. If you want to go higher, be inclusive, not exclusive. Learn a little. Be open to more, and you will do more. And remember, you will do more together than you will alone. So, pick your team strategically.

There is power in numbers, so create a team that empowers you. Create a team that you empower. Synergize your success.

Don't Wait for Opportunity—Create It
opportunity
/opportunity/
noun

a set of circumstances that makes it possible to do something

You landed your dream job! It must be fate! Wrong—so wrong. I have never been one to believe in fate or destiny. They always seem to be manufactured words to describe the not-so-mysterious things that happen to us. Being in the right place at the right time is not written in the cards. It is not your destiny. For whatever reason, you just happened to be where you were. And while you were there you made the most out of it because you had the skill set and the desire to do so.

Possibility stems from circumstance. Baker would not have been formed if it were not for the fact that David, Joel, and I had been working in close proximity to one another. (There you have it—the right place at the right time.) But, there's a catch—we all had what it took to be successful. If we did not each come in with our own strengths and skills, the idea never would have lifted off the ground.

You can be in any place that you want to be, but if

you do not have the skills to create the opportunity that you want, nothing is going to get off the ground.

That said, seek to immerse yourself in experiences that will make you more valuable and marketable so that when you do find yourself in, let's say a coffee shop, and you bump into a like-minded individual, you can work to bring an idea to fruition.

A lot of my life was spent creating opportunity for myself. I was hyperaware of the fact that I would need to possess certain traits to accomplish what I wanted to. Optics are everything. To run in the right circles and have the same access to opportunity as my more privileged peers I knew that I would have to appear a certain way— play a role so to speak. I am not saying that I "faked it till I made it." I loathe that advice—it is inauthentic and unproductive. I am saying that after careful introspection and self-awareness, I made a conscious decision to improve myself.

Duke was a blank canvas. It was an opportunity for me to start fresh in a place where there were not any preconceived notions of me. No one knew the high school version of me. It was nearly the polar opposite of the community I had known. I knew that I would be able to alter my optics and design myself to have traits that would help me to associate with the highest common denominators at Duke.

I coined the term "Roger by Design."

Part by part, idea by idea, I stitched together a newer version of myself—I was picky about what traits I wanted to keep and which qualities I needed to cultivate—this was my self-engineered transformation. As you can imagine, this alteration occurred intentionally and after careful introspection. This version always puts his best foot forward. In the workplace, people most commonly see "Business Roger," the pragmatic, focused, solution-based version of myself. This was the Roger I worked hard to design. This Roger indulged in seriousness and practicality. Yet, he was a leader who also practiced compassion as a companion for his coworkers. If there was a problem, he wanted to help his team solve it. He was intentionally empathetic as he worked to create a safe and comfortable environment for the people he worked with. This version of Roger was engineered to succeed.

I started this journey to self-design in college and have continued to develop it. Business Roger leveraged his experience and evolved over the years due in a large part to a fine balance between humility and malleability.

In high school I was an introvert, yet I knew that if I wanted to advance myself, I would have to force myself to be more of an extrovert. So, I did. I worked on it and coerced myself to meet more people. Sometimes I overcompensated for being introverted by being overtly extroverted. But it was this very action that allowed me to get out of my comfort zone and into the discomfort zone. The more I did this, the easier it became—I listened to my instinct and did the opposite, recognizing that it was the only way for me to grow. At times it was a challenge, but I love a good challenge—I always have. I made sure to dress the part of what I believed success to be, meticulously picking out coordinated outfits despite my color blindness.

I was hyperaware of anything that resembled a Jersey accent emanating from me, and so I worked diligently to rid myself of any trace. There is nothing wrong with a Jersey accent aside from the fact that people use it as an opportunity to place judgment on those who have one. I recognized that it held a negative connotation in the higher circles of society. I thought that ridding myself of my accent would put me in the best possible situation moving forward—and it did.

When I got to college, I surrounded myself with peers who wanted success as badly as I did, but knew how to temper their ambitions with their passions. A complete transformation requires a balance among all things, and so I learned that to be considered successful, I had to reconcile my drive with patience. I had to learn that all parts of people—their history, their heritage, their goals, their quirks—must transform together, synthesizing without deleting. I could alter parts of myself to gain the competitive edge, but I did not want to erase my distinctions to fit in. And that was the moment I realized that fitting in at Duke wasn't what was important. Instead, I wanted to grow up.

In reality, immersion was difficult. In the beginning, I felt out of place. Even isolated. I did not want people to know where I came from because I did not want my origins to be their first impression of me. It's not that I was ashamed. I just didn't want them to think that the Hispanic boy from South Hackensack had a background that felt too dissimilar, maybe too lacking, from theirs. Perhaps it was projection, but I didn't want to have to take the extra step of proving my worth, and so I shed my old skin.

Every change I have ever made in myself was calculated. I kept what worked, and I threw out what didn't. Each time I identified a perceived weakness I sought to change it. This extended beyond business. When I was a senior in college, I studied abroad in Australia where I found myself surrounded by hikers, surfers, and travel junkies. They were all walking around barefoot, manhandling the rough gravel with nothing but their skin. So, what did I do? I committed to walking around barefoot, and I did so for the entire semester, acquainting my callous-less feet to the harsh gravel. Where I was, walking around with shoes was burdensome, both to my efficiency and to the group to which I belonged, so I took them off. This isn't to say that I wanted to blend in; it is because I challenged myself to understand why their way was superior. So, I toughened up, and I blended in to fit my environment.

What I perceived as a weakness, became an intolerable trait. Maybe it was vulnerability, but I wasn't willing to turn a blind eye to it. To be perfectly honest, my "soft" feet might have been considered just that, and potential shortcomings were impediments to my growth. I had no room for them.

I want to make a distinction, however—I did not become calloused to anything—I honestly just wanted to weed out the traits, habits, and narrative that I told myself.

All my changes, even learning how to "thrive" while barefoot, were conscious. I changed both for a want and a need. Throughout my transformations, I never forgot where I came from. I just refused to let it define where I was going to go.

I have never been one to stay where the system told me to.

Not to mention, after my stint in Australia, I realized that I don't particularly like to stand still.

Run in the Right Circles

circle

/circle/

noun

a group of people with shared professions, interests, or acquaintances

You hear people say it all the time—so much of getting anywhere in life is a matter of who you know. Yes, hard work plays a role, but sometimes you can work as hard as you want and never get a break while the guy right next to you walks through the open door because he "knows a guy."

We all want to know a guy who knows a guy. Better yet, we want to be the guy whom everyone wants to know.

Knowing "the guy" is a testament to the network you have built, where the respect, notoriety, and empirical value that you have created delivers options.

Weaponize your network. Make it work for you.

One of the reasons I chose to go to such an esteemed university was because of the people who went there. Duke has a reputation for its elite culture. People who go to Duke go on to do big things. Naturally I knew this, and I wanted to be a part of the culture that they created there, which transcended campus lines. The college has a ring to it. As far as perceptions go, if you go to Duke, you are "elite" and intelligent—again another stamp. I know how this can be perceived: "That is exactly what is wrong with the idea of 'elitism.'" I agree—it is wrong to judge a book by its cover, but not because Duke does anything that doesn't merit their phenomenal perception—they craft and cultivate a culture and campus that deserve the accolades they receive. They encourage success. They create an ecosystem that provides an apparatus to help you achieve, not deter you.

To give you an example: through association with me, my father faced judgment in the workplace. As a woodworker who served the community, his business model was naturally and intentionally centered around family. My dad facilitated close connections with his customers by virtue of his personal interactions and the products that he created for them. By the mere act of creating what he did, kitchen cabinets, for example, he became part of their daily lives. The cabinets were a product of his creation, his work, and his vision; they were products of passion that he shared with his customers.

It was common for him to allow me to accompany him on jobs, and because of this, a lot of his clients knew me. My dad, upon my admission to Duke, proudly told a client of this. And at that very admission, he became more of a peer to the client. He was not seen so much as a woodworker who was hired by a privileged client, but as someone who worked, just as the man who had employed him, to raise a family. And more than that, he was seen as a man who instilled values in children that made them capable of attending a university such as Duke. This one client in particular could not stop talking about it. Looking back now, I imagine the idea the client must have had of my dad and his family. That always struck me, that others "othered" me. This was an eye-opening realization for me. As soon as those words left my dad's mouth, he too had been stamped (just by association with me). We became "that family" in his mind. This is how society works, we are "guilty by association." We are defined by labels that we did not assign to ourselves. My father's clients had known him for years. He had a strong relationship with them and still, when they heard "Roger got into Duke" they pegged him as "That dad who has a son who is at Duke." What this means to you may be different than what it means to me or someone else. I know my story (and now you do too). I was not the typical kid who gets into Duke. I was a rare statistic and yet people (such as my dad's clients) created a story in their minds that fit the label that society has put on Duke. If you go to Duke, you must be highly intelligent, white, privileged, and elitist, right? Your summer must be spent in the Hamptons, right? Wrong. This is a generalization; it is not the truth, and it expands to nearly every realm of life. Labels are generalized versions of reality, they are not the truth.

College was everything that I planned and needed it to be. Throughout my twenty years in business, the contacts I made at Duke served as references for me, helping me to network and cross bridges that I otherwise may not have ventured. Duke was a place where I met new ideas and shared my own with circles of like-minded individuals. It was a place where for the first time, I felt that I was meeting people who could be a part of my tribe.

My journey to get here was iterative, but also intentional. I continued to grow, change, and develop. Each evolution, whether small or large, led to an improved version of myself. I deliberately chose to focus.

My choices, intentional or lucky, led me to open my mind, my circle, and my opportunities. Kids from my culture and neighborhood were not expected to run in big circles, and they oftentimes ran in the wrong ones. As a result, their futures weren't "bright," if they even existed at all.

In a lot of ways, their outcomes were the result of poverty, bad luck, and fewer opportunities to make better choices. Access to proper funding and education could have prevented more of them from falling into the wrong crowd, and the statistics say that it would have.

Access to quality education and career paths are

inalienable rights. This is the United States, after all. We are built on the concept of equality meeting effort to serve an almost insatiable need for success. If we were to implement this foundational concept, then the system would stop passing out ladders to "deserving" individuals. Instead, we would all get in an elevator to move up the floor together. Yes, capitalism has its issues—it encourages competition at all costs—but it also is a stairway to a better life. If we divorce the steps from the journey and replace them with elevators, the learning experience of life is missed. This is my gripe with so-called social equity programs that aren't designed to answer the one question that must be posed: how do we change the system, not solve for its downfalls?

Growing up in South Hackensack, I lived across the street from Memorial Park where I spent afternoons playing soccer or basketball. Directly across the park in one of the many quintessential Italian suburban homes that surrounded us lived Carmine. I mentioned we lived in mob country, right?

Carmine was my classmate and a year older than I. He was the consummate class clown, likely his way of coping with being held back a grade. He was an incredibly intelligent student who transformed himself into the class clown out of boredom. His mind could have run circles around most of our peers; he just didn't apply himself. Carmine, unlike me, fit in to the largely Sicilian community of South Hackensack. His family was always very nice to my family, and our mothers were fairly good friends. This is noteworthy only because years later I found out that when my parents first moved into South Hackensack they were told in no uncertain terms that they had no problem kicking people out of town whom they didn't like. Fortunately, my parents are likeable folks.

You see, my family was one of the first families not of Sicilian descent to move into South Hackensack. If you didn't grow up in the Northeast or haven't ever watched The Sopranos (shame on you!) then what I'm trying to tell you is that there was a certain organized portion of the community that was ever present but seldom visible.

I don't remember now how I found out, but when I was thirteen, I learned that Carmine would not be returning to school. Why? Carmine was dead; a victim of a self-inflicted gunshot wound to the head in his parent's garage. I felt numb when I heard the news. At the age of thirteen I needed to evaluate my mortality. Carmine's funeral was the first and last funeral I have ever been to. I remember walking up to the casket and seeing my friend's body, lifeless. I didn't know how to process it. I sat down and cried into my hands for what might have been minutes but could have been an hour. I kept trying to figure out why. How could a person who was so genuinely jovial be driven to take his own life?

I have always had a difficult time with religion; seeing it as more of a crutch to hide from reality than a belief system. Growing up Latino there was no choice in the matter. I was stamped "Catholic" on the forehead the minute I arrived on March 14, 1978. Ever since then I was always questioning my religion. As somebody who, even as a young person, valued empirical proof over all else, the numbers never added up for me. In a lot of ways, I think Carmine's death was the last nail in the coffin for any semblance of belief that I had once had. I just could not accept that this was "God's plan" or however you might put it.

I remember being young and thinking that life could end in a moment—this epiphany was one of the reasons I took advantage of everything I did. From this experience, something that I learned was to remind myself of the following: You never know when this ride will come to an end, so if there are things you want to do, you'd better get started. To think that self-motivation came out of this incredibly sad event puts a small smile on my face.

Later on, I found out more details around the circumstances of Carmine's death. Granted, this was small-town gossip mill fodder so take it for what it is. The whispers revealed that Carmine had been involved with some members of the nefarious organized community

I mentioned earlier. Apparently, he had been a runner of sorts. As the story goes, he lost something. He lost something very valuable. Rather than letting his family be hurt by this group of people I mentioned (the ones who get back at you by getting to your family), he decided to take it upon himself to pay the price.

Being confronted with the death of a close friend, especially considering the circumstances around that death, really makes any sort of fairy-tale living fade into the background. I came away from this experience a little less innocent and with more resolve to be the master of my own destiny. I wouldn't let myself be a statistic. I'd do everything I could to stack the cards in my favor. I knew that if I didn't transform this horrible experience into a life well lived, then the efforts of my parents and my own instincts would have been wasted.

I vowed to respond instead of react. Reactions mean emotion. Responses mean careful calculation. Coupled with that promise, I made it a rule to pick my circles wisely and to transcend my circumstance in every way possible.

Level the Players, Not the Field
level
Ilevell
adjective

at the same height as someone or something else

I was one of only a few students from my high school to attend Duke without an athletic scholarship. Four years prior to my acceptance, one student had gone there to play football. While I am proud of this accomplishment, my point in telling you about it is to help paint a picture of where I came from. People from my area did not go to Ivy Leagues or Stanford's or Duke's unless their athletic achievements could afford them the opportunity. The person I have in mind actually came from a more privileged background than mine, but were it not for his athletic achievement, he wouldn't have been able to meet the high barrier of entry. My high school was located in a suburb outside the inner city—funding was low, and the socioeconomic status of the attendees was even lower. This did not equate to a quality education, which all too often is the case. You know the saying, the rich get richer and the poor get...poorer. There is no hiding the fact that our system is not designed for the bottom to rise—it is tiered. Without access to the same quality education and experiences, how can minorities in low socioeconomic areas ever access the same opportunities as their wealthy counterparts in neighboring districts?

The truth is, they can't, unless they have the desire to seek it out themselves. Of course, this requires doing more than the people at the top and breaking patterns ingrained deep within the core of society. It requires breaking out of the mentality of your tribe and defining success in your own way. Additionally, it requires an awareness of your circumstance and an understanding that there is more to life than the boundaries into which you were born.

Don't get me wrong here—I am not saying that we need to level the playing field. I am saying that we need to level the players who go there. We need to create a world where there is equal access to opportunity. The only way to do that is to give everyone access to the tools they need to succeed.

We are not all equal. We are not born into the same exact circumstance with the same access to education and opportunity.

The reality is we are not all going to be rich. We are not all going to be poor. We are not all going to create billion-dollar companies, but we should all have equal access to opportunity in order to do so (if we so wish).

To make this a reality, we need to be able to A) be aware of this reality, and B) know what we need to have in our toolbox. I would like to think that one day the system will change, and minority kids born into poverty will have everything they need to rise, but right now it is not on the horizon—funding is too low, and the system is banking on the suppression.

The world is not going to put tools in your toolbox—you need to go out and get them yourself. It is important to note that the tools I need may not be tools that you need. To be clear, when I talk about tools, I am not talking about wrenches. I am talking about immersing yourself into experiences, programs, and classes to help to narrow the gap.

I did.

When I first heard about an inclusion program in my area, I vividly remember thinking, "why not"? I always had an internal struggle with programs (like this one) that were designed to help minority communities get a "leg up" on the privileged class. But I grew up in the era of affirmative action—which I did not align with, in its original incarnation, because it conflicted with my devotion to meritocracy, but the fact is, taking advantage of the tools available to me was the intelligent thing to do. Advancing the value of these programs was then, and is now, a critical social imperative. We need an apparatus that equally dispenses education and exposure, and perhaps most importantly, provides support, so that our dreams don't need to be just dreams.

Our dreams could be earned.

I've always believed that advancement should be based on merit. Don't get me wrong. I understand why the program was put in place, but I've always wanted to be recognized for my abilities and not have any asterisks by my name as to why I was in the room in the first place.

There were two parts to my experience in one of these programs. First, there was the nonprofit organization that was in charge of the placement and the "training" that was intended to give everyone in the program as much of a chance at success as possible. The second part to this experience was my internship at Lucent Technologies, which I obtained through the nonprofit organization.

The nonprofit and my internship were almost totally opposed in their narratives, and I learned vastly different things from each.

From the beginning, I felt it was not likely that I would learn a lot from the placement and training team at the nonprofit. The lessons they were trying to teach from day one seemed very basic to me. While knowing how to speak respectfully, dress professionally, and tailor your language to your audience struck me as elementary, it was novel information for many others.

Looking back, I don't know what I was hoping I would learn. But I expected it to be something other than social business cues that anybody could learn from watching enough television. I did not realize it then but as I reflected on this experience, I realized that I was trying to align at the HCD while everyone else seemed comfortable on the tier upon which they stood. I did not want to engage in this small talk, I wanted to start having big conversations.

My time at Lucent Technologies was different. I did not have an asterisk by my name like I did at the nonprofit, despite the fact that everyone knew that I was the minority intern. I was good with computers, self-assertive, and driven—I think that my mentors there saw this. I enjoyed the freedom to be who I was without a label, and they were grateful to have a hard-working intern.

What I have learned is this—these programs can be necessary for some kids. Not everyone picks up on the subtleties regarding presentation in the way that I did. Knowing how to dress and how to speak are learned behaviors, and if you are learning from people (namely your parents, other family members, or people in your community) who do not know the professional business world, chances are that you won't be as prepared.

It goes without saying that kids born into privilege don't need to go this extra mile. Knowing how to speak and dress are already in their tool boxes. Why? Because they were born into circumstances in which success, and all its facets, were not just visible, but a lifestyle. As a function of their optics and access, they don't typically have to jump the hurdle of trying to define what success looks (or dresses) like. Internships, then, are commonplace in their academic lives, and in fact, are often normal experiences in their upbringing.

It is already expected that they will be an intern in their family's company. (Perhaps this is a gross generalization, but it is also a part of our reality.) There is nothing to sugarcoat here. It is not right or wrong. It just is. What I am trying to say is that these opportunities are already offered to the privileged and they aren't to "people like me." People like me saw grit and hard work, but they did not see high society. Likewise, the privileged kids may not have shared in my work ethic because they did not have to, yet I may not have shared in their access to opportunity because of my circumstances. Necessity is based on circumstances. What I needed, the others did not. And vice versa.

Pursue Happiness
happiness
/happiness/
noun

the state of being happy

If the dictionary cannot define "happy" as a one-size-fits-all, I am not sure that I can. Nor can I say for sure that happiness even exists. What I can say is that we have every right to seek it out.

I often visited Costa Rica in my youth—as an adult my perspective shifted even more. Even landing at the airport, the disparity between being a lower-middle-income American and a poor Costa Rican was a massive chasm, and their perception of our "wealth," however unfounded in reality, was understandable. Their mentality always seemed to be *money grows on trees where you come from. Your life must be easier. That's why you have more.* They did not understand that my family's success, and that of the others they solicited, was the result of hard work and difficult decisions that not a lot of people are willing to make.

I remember thinking—if you want "this" (possession, opportunity, life), go and get it. The only thing stopping you is your circumstance and the singular perspective you have because of it. Yes, people have certain life situations. While we are not free from the consequences of our choices, we are free to choose how we want to live our lives. I chose how to live my life, and I followed a path that made me happy. When a circumstance stopped serving me—I changed it. This speaks to an earlier point, but it is valid here as well. We have the right to live our lives however we want to. Need more proof? Look no further than the blueprint of the United States.

Per the Constitution, we have the freedom to engage in the pursuit of happiness; the right to seek opportunity that will lead to our version of contentment. We are not guaranteed happiness—that is not written in our Constitution. Instead, we are told that we can spend our lifetimes striving to obtain it. The irony of course is that we are never even told that happiness exists at all.

Assuming that happiness does exist, it is a lot like success. We all define it differently. What makes you happy is not what makes me happy. Yet despite our individual versions of "happiness," there is a universality in the concept that we don't all note. It is OK to be different. In fact, it is better to be different. Imagine a world where we all strived to obtain the same goals that would lead to our contentment. It would be boring, undiversified, and unevolved. If we all wanted to be businesspeople, there would be no musicians, teachers, or writers. We would have businesses but no one to construct the buildings, curate the marketing, or do the copywriting. Businesses would not be able to function. My point being, there is a reason that we all have different things that make us happy. Pursue a life that speaks to you.

Define Success

success

|success|

noun

the accomplishment of an aim or purpose

Success is a hunger driven by motivation and steered by single-mindedness and self-awareness. It is perhaps one of the most difficult ways to conduct your life, because it is almost myopic in its needs, but I was hungry for more. Yet all human beings who have desires, or ambitions, or want a chance at whatever success they seek, shares that same appetite—the only difference is the commitment to foraging or hunting.

Success is a moving target. As you grow, so too does your definition of achievement. As you fail, so does the barometer of your definition evolve. Success is not a point in the space/time continuum—it is dynamic enough that our experience can either expand or contract its meaning to our lives. To me, success is a marker—a goal that aligns with your opportunity meeting its target. It is the accomplishment of your efforts, needs, and passions. Naturally, this is different for everyone. Some people, especially ones from my town defined success as holding a stable job—say a teacher or a tradesman—and remaining as comfortable as possible. There was, and is, nothing wrong with this—it was just not for me. It did not fit my version of success.

Before you set out to create opportunity, take a moment to define what success means to you—set your metric and really define what you want. Is it putting dinner on the table every night? Is it starting your own business? Take a deep look at what you want and make a list of what you need to get there. Education? Capital? A job? Set the metric, and start planning.

Every destination has a path. If it doesn't, forge one. If it does, follow it. And remember, setbacks are not just common, they are expected. Your definition of success may oscillate based upon your setbacks, but that should not take you off course. Remember, your direction is toward success and if an obstacle changes the shape of that, your metric may change but your goal of being successful does not have to. Once you know this, you will embrace the bumps in the road more than dread them. My metric for success was starting my own company. I cannot say exactly what led me to this conclusion. I just knew that it was my goal. My mom always told me that I was like my father in that I would be better off working for myself. She was right, but the funny thing is that once you start working for yourself and being an entrepreneur, you end up working for other people. The difference is that you work with them (and for them), but not under them.

Once I defined my metric, I had to make sure that I had the qualifiers to attain it. So, I took a good hard look in the mirror. First, I assessed the tools that I already had and made a mental list of traits and tools that I needed to acquire. For example, I knew that I was good at coding, but in order to climb the ladder I needed to be able to do more and know more. So, I worked to improve my public speaking, I honed in on techniques for market analysis, and I learned the importance of building company culture. But, I knew that none of this would matter if I did not immerse myself into the role of a self-starting businessperson.

So, I did not just "play" the part, I became the part, authentically and wholly, dressing and speaking to fit my metric. Regardless of your metric, you can do this too. Look in the mirror, think about what values you already have and analyze where you can improve.

It was my definition of success that defined where and what I wanted and where I wanted to go. I put an X on the map, I made a list of what I needed, and I did not stop until I got where I wanted to go.

Indulge Your Practicality

practical

/practical/

adjective

(of an idea, plan, or method) likely to succeed or be effective in real circumstances; feasible

The people closest to me know that my mind-set is solution oriented and cerebral—I like to call this trait "logical." At times, however, my pragmatism gets misconstrued for a total lack of emotion. And while I am not devoid of feelings, I rely more heavily on facts (especially in the realm of business and personal growth). In my opinion, emotion clouds judgment that pragmatism can handle. If there is a problem, there is a solution. You just need to be willing to do what it takes to get there. This is the black-and-white part of life. We make it gray with our emotion and indecisiveness, overcomplicating scenarios that require tasks we do not want to face. Take my dad, for example. Before he jump-started his woodworking business he worked in the oil and gas industry. He disliked the field and made a calculated decision to change it. He knew that he was passionate about woodworking, and he knew that he wanted to change careers. Naturally, he had emotions around this, but he did not let his emotions influence a rash or impulsive decision. He did not up and leave his stable job on a whim. He started working two jobs, taking on woodworking clients on top of the job that he already had. He made a commitment to get where he wanted to go, but he laid out a smart path to do so, one that allowed him to support his family and build up a client list that would allow him to support his family and continue planning for their future. There was every possibility that he could have failed, but he didn't.

It is important that we delineate between emotions and passion. They are not one in the same. Emotions are feelings derived from circumstance; passion is a sentiment that inspires you to elevate your circumstance.

Emotions serve a purpose in the working world— they can heighten experiences with insight and passion, both of which fuel our commitment to our decisions. Emotions, if not balanced, can rid us of logic—A/B choices, for example, that require our focus— and we can end up making what I call "feel-good" decisions. These choices are the exciting ones, the ones we make without thinking. While making a reactive decision may seem "instinctual" at the time, it often sets us up for conflict or failure later on down the road. When we color our world with the lens of wistfulness of making a hope a reality, we shortcut our path. These shortcuts divorce pretty critical points—learning experiences; being faced with, and then making hard decisions, and finding the tenacity in ourselves to align heart with mind.

Balance is important in life. It is critical to be able to leverage opposing or conflicting ideals. A great example of this, in my opinion, is in picking a career. So often we go to one-sided extremes, figuring that our choices have to be all-or-nothing. When really, it is more about finding a way to leverage what we want and what we need.

I believe that you should follow your passion… so long as it is a practical one. I want to be clear here— practicality and passion are not mutually exclusive. Your practical sense can also be passionate.

When I was eleven, I started to work with my father. I did not realize it then, but he had mastered the balance between passion and pragmatism. I learned practical skills, but I also learned about the importance of self-sufficiency and a strong work ethic.

My father had a love for his craft that I always admired. As you know by now, when my dad first immigrated to the United States he worked in the oil and gas industry. Yet, he did not like the hours he had to work or the lack of autonomy (which he craved) so he fell back on a trade that he knew well—woodworking. He harnessed his skill set and found a practical way to apply it. He found a way to make his passion work for him.

My dad oftentimes takes credit for my decision to

major in computer science, encouraging me to develop those skills. At first, I ignored his direction and majored in electrical engineering. I was always strong in math and science, and I thought it was something that would be in line with my passions.

I was wrong. I did not like circuits, and my hat's off to the people who do.

As fate would have it, Introduction to Computer Science was a prerequisite for engineering. The course and Owen Astrechan, the professor who taught it, made a lot of sense to me. Dr. Astrechan taught in a way that made dense content digestible, so digestible that I started to enjoy not only the lectures, but the theory behind the logic. So, I switched majors and did a BA instead of a BS. For me, this choice was logical—I knew that I did not need a BS because a future on the academic side of computer science was not something that I wanted. And choosing to obtain a BA would open up time for me to get an art degree—something that I had always been passionate about. I knew that art was not practical, but I found a way to insert practically into it.

My minor in visual design allowed me to indulge my passion in a logical way. And when the dotcom bubble burst, it ended up being my saving grace; many of my friends lost their jobs, but because of my art background I did not meet the same fate. In the world of development, visual talent is just as valuable as programming. It made me a more valuable asset.

While I loved drawing, I did not major in it. Why? It was a risk that I could not rationalize, a risk that was unlikely to lead to the optionality that I craved. So, why get a minor in an art field? Well, because it enhanced my skill set and made me more marketable; it made me better at what I was already doing. When I took a course in web design, I learned quickly that I could rationalize a degree in visual design because it would improve my skill in website design. This was how I found my balance.

You may hear some people say things like "follow your passion" and "do what makes you happy." These people often get deemed the idealists. Others, the so-called realists, will tell to find a job that supports you regardless of whether or not it makes you happy. Personally, I believe in finding the intersection between these polar ends of the spectrum, and my degree choices are a testament to that. I wanted to make my passion work for me.

To strike this balance, you need to take time to understand your passion. What are you passionate about? What is passion, anyway? And what does following that passion mean for your future? Will your passion open doors in your career? These are all important questions to ask yourself.

My freshman-year roommate was extraordinarily

bright. He chose to focus on medieval studies. I remember wondering what he would do with that major. What opportunity would await him after graduation? Would he become a teacher? Get a PhD? What else could he do with that degree if his metric of success were to shift? Unless he found a way to think outside the box, he would likely be limited in his options. What circles will he run in? As we discussed above, the circles that we run in are critical indicators of how high we can climb. I could not help but think that his network in that field might not offer him the potential to create options that might seem peripheral to his degree, or conversely, completely unassociated with his education versus expand his choices. At the end of the day, if becoming a teacher was his metric of success (and I am not saying that there is anything wrong with that), then his major was a part of his trajectory to get there. But, what if after teaching for years, he no longer wanted to be a teacher? What other options would he have? Probably not many. I could never come to terms with the idea that a choice could limit me; I never wanted to be suffocated by limitations. I believe in optionality; in fact, I crave it. I want to know that my choices possess the potential to open many doors, not just one. I want to know that any path I walk down has the potential to lead me down multiple rabbit holes of infinite opportunity.

I want you to do the same: are your choices binary,

or are they versatile?

While I have used college degrees as an example here, this mentality is one that transcends the undergraduate years. If I am being honest, most degrees (other than medical or engineering ones, generally speaking) open the door to your first job, but come time for exploration, diversification, or expansion of your skill set, the burden of securing a position to align with your broader view is placed squarely on your shoulders. Your values, whatever they may be, in synergy with your drive, will lead you to your subsequent positions. For clarity's sake: the job market, your ability to interview well, your job performance in current and past roles, and your network will also be deciding factors in your career placement. When the time to elevate your career and network comes, reconcile your reality with your passion.

I say this often, but every step along your personal and professional journey will require a continued commitment to this philosophy. It evolves only when you do, so I urge you to create, implement, and execute a litmus test for your most critical decisions in life that, if chosen correctly, will lead to more. More options, more opportunities, and more experiences. These branches stem from a mind-set rooted in growth.

Gain an Advantage

advantage

/advantage/

noun

a condition of circumstance that puts one in a favorable or superior position

Haves and have-nots. I prefer do's, and do-nots. Cheesy, and maybe even too black and white, but the fact is we must accept the reality of life and then do our best to alter it in our favor. There will always be someone who has an advantage, either by birth or by design, but don't let those levels deter you—let them motivate you to become that person. To gain an advantage, you must put yourself into the best possible situation, because opportunity waits for no one. Leveraging isn't about climbing on the backs of others or forcing the hand of society. It is about transforming your experiences into lessons that catalyze your abilities. I tried living by this philosophy during my time at Duke. The connections that I formed expanded—not only my network of people, but my ecosystem of thoughts. With these new tools, I entered into the world of start-ups. I met people from many backgrounds and the diversity I encountered expanded my scope of experience, even if I lived vicariously through the lifestyles of others.

By observing their habits, their values, and their choices, I realized a powerful truth—access to information, at every level, is imperative.

Gaining an advantage is a matter of access—access to education, funding, and tools that will lead to more success. Of course, access stems from the modalities I just described, but it also derives from whom you know. Knowing the right people can be the difference between shaking hands with success or closing the door on it. This access comes more easily to some of us than it does to others. Some people are born into it; others have to work for it. If it wasn't clear—I had to work for it. And while I was not born into privilege, I had different advantages from my upbringing, ones that I utilized as tools to elevate myself.

I was born into a family who taught me the importance of hard work, tenacity, and charisma. I was born into a family who showed me the importance of building relationships. I was born into a family who taught me to always put my best foot forward. So, while there was no easy path to get where I wanted to go, I was fortunate to have everything I needed. I learned that shiny objects don't always glitter if the right light isn't shone on them. To reflect success, you need to see beyond the surface of what seems possible. You have to be willing to leverage your vision.

In my journey, the unchanging variable remains this: I don't want, or expect, or respect, a world that hands me anything.

It is true—there are severely underserved, underrepresented, and maligned segments of society. Those whose access to opportunity is crippled, if it exists at all.

But there is a great equalizer—desire. Whatever that means to you, whether it is success, survival, or notoriety, it doesn't detract from the passion that serves desires.

So, I say again—in my life, and in the lives of my peers, we have to choose our path—not demanding all opportunities be created equally, but that access to those opportunities is equal.

Equal access to opportunity, not equal opportunity for all.

As always, you have to make a choice.

WE ARE NOT BINARY
by GREG VIRGIN

Greg Virgin is the founder and CEO of Redjack, and has dedicated both his professional career and his passion to the protection of information. Redjack currently monitors over 8% of the Internet's public IP space and over 40 trillion business communications per year through their proprietary product, but it is his personal and company mission to empower diverse technology environments. His dedication to social equity, human liberty, and data-driven insights has led him to create platforms, voices, and safety nets for those whose voices have been muffled. Greg continues to commit his time to securing our world and our ideas.

The world is not binary.

We are not one, or the other. Our identities, our roles, and our convictions, they evolve, iterate, and grow.

Human beings are imperfect, and so, identities that we cling to don't always reflect our sum totals. Even then, so many of us hold onto them nonetheless.

Being a twin, however, wasn't the easiest identity to

shed – my name even is a mirror of my brother. When I asked my dad, "Why, why would you name us…" wait for it, "Greg Scott and Scott Greg?" His response was pretty logical: "Well, we conceived you once so why should we have to name you twice?" Coupled with our matching childhood outfits and perhaps most surprisingly, our memories, (we recall, as a twin-set, what we experienced, but can't identify which one of us actually went through it,) I didn't know who I was outside the borders of my shared identity.

We were one, despite being two.

So, when it came time to construct an individual version of myself, I looked beyond the borders of my tribe. Naturally, my brother did the same, as do we all when the time to forge our identity comes. I needed to attach to ideas and things that defined me, not my place in the family unit, or the neighborhood, or society.

I gravitated to open circles, not closed ones.

I realized, however, that my brain was broken when it came to accepting the concept of identity – I didn't, and don't align with tribal mentalities – in fact, I avoid them entirely. The concept of attaching based solely on gender, race, or region, is to me, such a narrow way of experiencing the world.

We are stronger together. The ways in which we operate beyond these socially imposed tribal traits, beyond gender and race, for example, compel us to expand our selves, and in doing so, the circles around us.

Despite the difficulties of growing up in an environment where my family's financial situation changed from upper middle class to barely scraping by, (there were a number of times I didn't know how I was going to eat. I remember families from my school all brought us honey baked hams… which was all I ate for like a week. I'm certainly alone in that I have both a starvation story and ski trip stories); despite experiencing the tragedy of a father who died due to a lack of equitable or even humane health care; watching my single mother who went through breast cancer and radiation therapy while never missing a day of work, to the point that her body had absorbed the maximum amount of radiation that the human body can withstand; despite those things that are unfair about being a human being, I learned that handling a diverse set of challenges and threats was the only real set of values that I wanted to align with, both from myself and from my new tribe.

This is the value of your network. My ability to cope with challenges is deeply influenced by the diversity of my circle, which continues to expand, iterate, and grow.

Like it, I also grow, expand, and iterate.

This formation, and forging, of the new self, is the ultimate hack – and that is where I intersected with Roger.

We didn't fit in with the established pedigree at Duke, because fitting in meant trying to get a seat at the table to represent our needs. We didn't need a seat at any table, because striving to achieve a higher purpose isn't about elevating the self, it is about elevating your perspective.

Why did I want to reach higher in life? Perhaps facing the mortality of my father, and almost my mother, and even, perhaps my own at six years old with a melanoma scare, these faces of mortality that I faced so early in life bred an urgency, almost primal need to meet some purpose, or even be worthy of success. I didn't die, I must have lived for a reason, I thought - there must be some purpose to this. I had a fire in my heart, and it seemed Roger shared the same compulsion to strive despite our difficulties. So much of it came down to purpose - creating one, finding one, and working towards one.

He, like many, is the guy who looks for opportunities. The difference, however, is that he hits the timing of availing of them well, because of one key distinction: he is open-minded. He sees potential, or maybe he sees something that might have potential, and because of his willingness to transform the less-than into something with a purpose, with a value higher than when he found it.

This quality is incredibly powerful, because it takes into account what worked for him in his life, and diminishes that which has worked against him.

Whether you come from nothing, or everything, moving forward cannot be an us versus them mentality. Success, although a personal journey, is easier, more enlightening, and more efficient if your higher purpose is to elevate your perspective. On that spectrum, color, gender, your economic status - it can't be seen. At Redjack, inclusion, and representation of diversity on our team is an infallible way of life. We are stronger together because we can operate beyond the constraints of our differences, and align on our shared perspectives, goals, and values. I have always felt that it isn't the ratio of men to women, or white to black, or any other arbitrary comparison - it is about the connection between groups that forms a better outlook, and more engaging life. To say that minorities need a seat at the table of success, a success that has been defined by one segment of society is almost categorically wrong. I don't think anyone, whether they come from a minority background or a disadvantaged one, should seek any seat at any existing table. Our goal should be to look beyond the table, the status quo - and have the audacity of autonomy.

I aim to include, not only because it is the smart choice, but because it is the right choice. Connection exists beyond the frontal cortex - it originates in the many facets of the mind. It is colored by experience.

Decisions, experiences, even identities, aren't black

and white. They grow, iterate, and evolve.

The world isn't binary.

Nor are we.

CHAPTER 3

DO YOUR RESEARCH

Diversity, as well as social justice programs, are valuable tools in finding the right answers to and powerful questions: what is the goal of understanding the truth? Why do we attempt to understand our reality, and in doing so, change it? What does inclusion really mean? We can't hide from the insights we gain as we honestly walk through the questions. Our collective truth is our strength. It provides humility as we build teams of the most varied set of perspectives. From gender to race to belief systems, our vantage points fortify our ability to leverage the experiences that shaped us. Like cannabis we are better when our communities are chosen based on a shared set of values born from a different set of understandings. The truth is the ability to empower ourselves.

***

Knowledge is possessing information.

Wisdom is utilizing it.

Research is the method that allows information to be sifted, tested, and then leveraged.

If you want to truly know anything, then start by researching it.

Carmine, my grade school class-mate and I were similar in one key trait—we both not only questioned authority, we were rarely satisfied with a complacent or placating explanation. We needed to know why, how, what to accept as an answer, and move forward. He questioned the world around him and seldom took what he was told at face value. I admired this about him, perhaps because he was the only other person I knew who was as inquisitive as I. I like the word inquisitive, but perhaps the word irritating is more appropriate. 'Why' was my constant companion - I needed to dig deeper, gain insight, and find an explanation. Unfortunately, the burden of irritation fell squarely on the exasperated adults that were incessantly bothered. I never understood why.

As humans, we use our senses to navigate our physical world. But we use our faith, that which we are told, to satisfy our curiosity about life, or norms, or beliefs. It is hard to fault ourselves for this; our brains are hardwired this way for our survival. Yet, we need to bring awareness to this fact and know that not everything we are told is the truth. I am going to urge you to question the world around you; to question what you are told, and more importantly to do your own research to find the facts.

A lot of getting where you want to go is a matter of optics. I talked about this already. But, how do you know the accepted standards for the optics you are trying to achieve? You have to put in the research. I did not learn how to dress from my parents (though they were snappy dressers). I learned how to dress from the shows I watched and from the businessmen I saw walking on the streets. I paid attention to these details, and I watched with intention. These people were successful. These successful people wore certain outfits. They carried themselves a certain way. Their verbiage was specific, to the point, and at times charismatic. They spoke with the intention of adding constructive feedback to the conversation. The real professionals did not try to cover their asses, they risked being on the border of unintentionally insulting. Each time I observed, took note, and emulated these traits, I was doing my research.

I did not always have to travel outside the walls of my home to do my research; some of the greatest input I ever received was from my dad.

My dad took care to interact with his customers on a personal level, taking time to check in with them about their health, their children, and their lives. He built relationships based on genuine care. If he was going to be late, he called and let them know. I got to see this at an early age, and I saw just how far that went.

He was not just genuinely invested in the well-being of his customers; he was also charismatic. While he had a charming personality, I think that his decision to incorporate charisma into his interactions at work was deliberate. The art of being charismatic is one that should be mastered; to be charismatic means that you can compel others into devotion with your enamoring personality. Charm is either innate or curated, but equally effective. My dad augmented his nature intentionally. As a result, he facilitated better relationships with his clients through his mannerisms, familiarity, and the way in which he spoke. On the off chance that he needed some leeway, he got it.

Of course, I did not realize it when I was younger, but nearly everything I saw my dad do with his work was seared into my brain. From watching my dad, I was able to collect data that proved to be useful to me as I entered the business world. When he chose woodworking as a career, I learned how to reconcile skill, passion, and need. From settling into a city that wasn't an enclave for immigrant Costa Ricans, I learned to break from the tribe to forge a personal path. From his work ethic, I learned the value of working smart, not just hard. From his intentional charisma, I learned the power of human connection in work.

I observed, so I learned. Think back, are there any influential lessons you learned from your own parents or guardians? If so, harness them and pat yourself on the back—you were doing research without even knowing it.

Research is not just important for your success, it is imperative. Use empirical evidence as a guiding force. Decisions in life should not be about what "feels" right or wrong or good or bad. Decisions should be calculated.

My point here is that you can take risks in life, you can do what you want, but you need to make sure that your choices are informed and that they play into the bigger equation for success. Remember, your choices should reflect what you seek to accomplish.

Don't Follow the Playbook
playbook
/playbook/
noun

a stock of usual tactics of methods

Equal access to information should be a fundamental human right. Without access, our ability to make informed choices is not just limited, it is crippled. The right inputs often determine our outputs. Case in point: our formative years—limited access to information in our adolescence is correlative to a lacking education system. This statement is obvious—the less you are taught, the less you learn. If you grow up in a low-income area there is less funding, which means less money to schools. Let's talk about application and implication (versus accumulation). Although curricula are standardized, the value of the application of information being taught in lower-income areas isn't designed to be leveraged for higher uses. We are not setting anyone up for success by asking them to memorize content and regurgitate facts. The purpose of a curriculum should not be to memorize but rather to engage in critical thought and practical skills that can carry over to life. The emphasis should be on skills, big ideas, and concepts, instead of recitation of the parts of a cell.

Now don't get me wrong. We can still find a way to provide that content in a beneficial way, but it should not be the emphasis. The vector through which we pose this content should be through the encouragement of skills such as communication and problem solving. We don't remember everything that we are taught; granular details go in one ear (if they make it there) and out the other.

This method of teaching that plagues our classrooms is a byproduct of circumstance and a system destined for failure. However, what happens when information isn't of applicable value, insight, or context? Our mentalities shift—we limit our ability to expand our horizons with new thoughts or diverse perspectives. With closed minds, we become rigid receivers of data, not dynamic participants in our learning. Yet when either a lack of information, misinformation, or information designed to mislead us enters our world, our closed minds cannot differentiate among the three.

Institutions create mind-sets, and mind-sets cycle to future generations. The terrible game of telephone that plagues us is both a function and a consequence of incomplete, un-empowering, and confining mind-sets that were shaped by a lack of access to unbiased, trustworthy, and complete information.

As I said, it is in our nature to believe what we are told by the people we are supposed to trust.

At an early age, we are thrown into a system of education. We sit in chair-filled rows, tethered to bells. When they ring (at the same time every day), we move. When they ring again, we sit. When the voice comes over the loudspeaker, we listen. When the PowerPoint comes on, we stare and take notes. We are told to pay attention. We are told that school is where we learn. We are told that knowledge is power and that education is the key to success. It is insinuated that if our knowledge is limited, so too are we. The irony, of course, is that the system is designed to keep us boxed into thoughts and norms that don't support analytical mind-sets.

Knowledge is not power.

The application of knowledge is powerful.

To entertain an idea without accepting it—that is intelligence.

Yet, there is a social safety in thinking alike.

We aren't taught to think critically. We are taught to

regurgitate information.

We aren't taught to make decisions. We are taught to parrot our teachers, whether they be society, media, or institutions.

How then, can we make autonomous decisions? How can we be expected to analyze, to ponder, to grow?

In our more formative years, we gain information through school, extracurricular activities, and life at home. Today we find ourselves in the age of the internet where nearly anything you want to know is at your fingertips. Thanks to search engines like Google, within seconds you can have answers to nearly any question you can fathom.

Keep in mind though, not everything on the internet is true. Nor is everything that you hear. Some information is intentionally skewed. Skewed to alter your system of beliefs in such a fundamental way that you may spend your entire life believing a lie to be a valid fact. That said, if you are not aware of this, you may never know a lie to be anything but a truth.

Our system is stacked against the liberty of information. Hidden beneath this disguise of freedom, we are influenced every day by the language we hear, the videos we see, and the words we read. And for what reason? Control.

Access to information is a fundamental right, yet it is taken from us every day without us knowing. Take cannabis for example—the so-called gateway drug. In middle school, DARE (Drug Abuse Resistance Education) representatives come into your classroom and tell you that drugs are bad. They tell you that cannabis is a drug that can kill you. They tell you that if you even think of consuming the plant, your entire world will be turned upside down, causing you to become addicted to heroin, lose all your friends, and succumb to a life on the streets (OK, so maybe I'm exaggerating, but you get the point). The bottom line is that they scare you out of any hope of liberty or optionality.

Drug propaganda tells us to stay away. YouTube censors educational cannabis content as does Google. Up until a few years ago, if you wanted a true education on cannabis, you needed to talk to someone in the industry who had been secretly operating in the darkness. Now you can go to apps such as Leafly and Weedmaps and receive access to educational and informative content. This content is transformative—allowing new and veteran users access to information they had never received before. And what is happening as a result? Views on cannabis are beginning to shift. More states are legalizing the plant, and talk of federal legalization is finally on the table. Why is this so important? Why do I wish to enlighten you on this matter?

Because access is not just important, it is essential.

We need to be informed in order to make proper decisions. We cannot make an educated choice if we do not know the facts. We not only need the facts, we deserve them, and we should demand them. If you cannot get the facts from somewhere or someone else, do your own digging. Conduct your own research. Experience everything you can, and collect data from those experiences. Follow empirical evidence, and don't take everything that you hear at face value. All too often there is more to the story, and you deserve to know what is on the missing pages.

I too have been fooled by the wrong information. I grew up in the Nancy Reagan "just say no" generation. Consequently, I believed that all drugs were bad. I bought into the propaganda that weed was a gateway drug. For the greater part of my youth, I stayed away from any opportunity to indulge in illegal substances. Like most people, I tried cannabis because my friends had access to it. Back then I would call it weed or pot; today I would refer to it as cannabis (times have changed).

I was eighteen when I first consumed cannabis. I could not tell you what strain I consumed. I could not tell you if it was Sativa, Indica, or a hybrid. Back then, you just smoked what you could get. I refer to these as the binary days of weed—you either had weed or you didn't. Anyway, my friend rolled a joint and passed it to me. I inhaled. This was big. I was ready for it. Life was going to be different.

I was pumped. Then, I exhaled…and nothing happened. I know what you are probably thinking. Roger—it was your first time and you did not inhale properly. I am here to tell you that I did inhale properly. But I literally felt nothing. This was absurd—where was the dangerous, transformative, or insane experience I had been sold? Years of propaganda from drug-education programs, Cheech and Chong movies, and just the general illegality of this "drug" had created such a massive illusion of pressure, or expectation, or fear, that I was honestly let down. How was this illegal? I felt more from a cup of coffee than a hit. I just didn't believe the effects to be significant enough to warrant cannabis being listed as a Schedule 1 drug. As the smoke from the plant flooded my system with almost zero impact on my behavior, I had a sudden and mind-blowing epiphany: I had been lied to. "What had I been afraid of?" If anything, the effects of alcohol seemed to me more "dangerous" and inhibiting than what I experienced, not just this first time but many times afterward. Empirically, alcohol has a consistent, measurable, and quantifiable effect. Consumed improperly, as is evidenced by its addictive nature, the epidemic of DUIs, and the massive industry that surrounds its responsible use, it is a substance that alters our interaction with reality.

Despite that, we are given the autonomy of using it as we wish. If anything, alcohol, and the culture surrounding it, are glamorized, even revered. It definitely isn't vilified as a recreational substance.

Early propaganda surrounding cannabis was perverse, ill intentioned, and irresponsible. For many, the constancy of the message completely brainwashed perspectives—and even worse, allowed ignorance to color decision making. Effectively, it eliminated our options. Had I grown up being told about the positive effects of cannabis and the mild high that results from consuming, I would not have been surprised by the experience I had. Yet, I was shocked. Shocked because my experience did not align with what I had been told for my entire life.

There is nothing to sugarcoat—we were all brought up and told what to think about cannabis. When you think about it, we are all brainwashed by our system. Brainwashed to think about drugs, school, laws, and work in certain ways. Every single thought that we are supposed to think is driven into our minds. All too often, we are too young to question what we are told. Our reference point is singular, and so, we buy what we are sold.

This transformative experience altered my understanding of my responsibility in making my own decisions. It is true, I did not have the opportunity or access to information from those who were supposed to teach. As a function of compulsion meeting curiosity, I studied the plant the only way I could—by just trying it for myself.

Had I never had this experience I would have continued to live my life with false institutional facts. So, I learned that the responsibility for awareness is on us. It is naive of us to think that the system is going to change. If it is true that history repeats itself, then we need look no further than our past to see where we are headed. And I guarantee, we are forging a path that we have walked before. We are walking in circles on the same path, beating our footprints into the ground.

As our world continues to shift, one thing is certain - we are responsible for doing our own research and for coming to our own conclusions. We cannot get so caught up in the entropy of change that we forget to rely on the facts.

We are at a critical time in society as the perception of the plant begins to shift. As people gain more information, the industry grows. As the optics surrounding the plant morph, the industry grows. When we talk about the shifting optics of the plant, we can look at the name as an example. The very decision to begin saying cannabis instead of weed helps people to shift their mentalities. Weed is something that you got from a dealer on the streets. Cannabis is a plant that you can legally purchase at your local dispensary for medicinal or lifestyle use. See the difference?

The newer generations are going to hear about

cannabis instead of weed. They are going to hear legal instead of illegal. Generations after them will begin to partake in this shift, without even knowing about it. Just as we hear about Prohibition and bootleggers today, they will hear about drug dealers and how the plant was once illegal. Of course, this is contingent on the continuous shifting of the optics of cannabis. Assuming that the alteration of the optics continues on this trajectory, there will be a more informed and positive shift toward cannabis and the importance of gathering one's own information in the future.

While shifting the optics of the plant is important, the more critical topic here is that the access people have to information needs to shift. Young people need to know the importance of doing their own research and having equitable access to information. The sharing of this knowledge is on us. We need to increase awareness about this topic so that a mass shift in mentality can happen.

My opinion on cannabis formed as a result of doing my own research. However, I think that having a conversation about whether cannabis is good or bad is an irrelevant conversation. Whether we are talking about cannabis, alcohol, or the pharmaceutical industry, people's opinions will differ. On a bigger scale, people are going to have differing opinions on everything in life. Some will say something is good. Some will say something is bad. I say, we are wasting our time focusing on this argument. If you want to form an opinion on cannabis (or anything in life), go out and try it yourself. My experience may not be your experience, and your experience may not be your neighbor's experience, and that is OK. This diversity adds color. Imagine what a boring world we would live in if everyone agreed.

It is important to reiterate that this good-or-bad argument goes beyond the topic of cannabis. People have this same debate about alcohol and the pharmaceutical industry. Ironically both of these industries are federally legalized despite the fact that many of their side effects are worse than those of cannabis. The negative effects of cannabis consumption do not measure up to those associated with a drug conjured from the pharmaceutical industry. Yet, we do not talk about that because the pharmaceutical industry is more accepted than cannabis distributors (at least in current times).

Right now, society is having assumption-based conversations. These conversations are turning into a game of telephone where he said this, and she said that, and no one quite knows what they are talking about. Even bigger than that, none of it is relevant because people are finding value in it. Regardless of whether they are consuming cannabis for medicinal purposes or because they just like the way that it feels, they value it.

Since cannabis is not legalized federally, large scale government funded research cannot be done. While we know some things, we also have a lot to learn. For example, we know about the endocannabinoid system, a system in our body involved in the function of our nervous and immune systems. We know about cannabinoids such as THC and CBD. We know about terpenes, aromatic oils that flavor cannabis. We know that cannabis can positively benefit users, especially those suffering from PTSD, pain, and anxiety. We also know that cannabis can benefit the everyday user who just wants to feel good.

While we can speculate from experience that cannabis has fewer negative side-effects than pharmaceutical drugs or alcohol, we do not have the data to back it up. I have to rely on my own experience and the evidence available to me to hypothesize that the effects of a pharmaceutical drug or alcohol could far outweigh the majority of the milder negative effects of cannabis. Take mortality rates for example. How many people have died from cannabis use alone? Zero. It is virtually impossible to overdose on it. How many people in the United States died from an opioid prescription overdose over the last two decades? Over two hundred thousand. How many people in the United States died from alcohol-related causes every year? Approximately ninety thousand. The numbers speak volumes to the consequences of consumption and yet cannabis's stigma still inhibits national legalization.

We need to do better. We need to push ourselves to have these bigger conversations. We deserve access to information about what is on the market so that we can make informed decisions for ourselves. Again, I am not saying that cannabis is good or bad. I am saying that we need to get all the information out in the open so that we can make our own educated decisions. The world is not going to tell you the truth. You have to define it for yourself. We need to put notes into our own playbooks.

I have said it before, and I will say it again. Language is a powerful display of optics. We hear that something is safe and legal and depending on who we hear it from, we think that it must be OK for us—we trust institutionalized information so the only modality of true change has to come from the top. We think that pharmaceutical drugs are OK for us because we trust the institutions that propagate them. We trust these institutions so we inherently trust that what they are offering is beneficial to our well-being.

Where is the moral high ground where we start holding people accountable for making uninformed decisions? It needs to exist somewhere in our system. One thing I have admired about Californians is that they have taken the road of empowerment and progress. Moral high ground. Lawmakers are beginning to make intentional choices that they are not going to support things that are negative for the health of California residents, regardless of the money an industry can bring in. Unlike Colorado, California had a conversation about liberty of usage and about diverting money from big tobacco to the cannabis industry. It is unfortunate that money has the power that it does. Yet, California is beginning the process of creating a nationwide wave of change.

Let's be honest, this lack of access to information has affected more people than just me. Unfortunately, it has disproportionately affected the poverty-stricken and minority segments of society. They have paid the price for a mentality that stems from mass misinformation.

Plant usage transcends race and gender. Millions of people worldwide use the plant for many reasons—some medical and some lifestyle. Regardless of their personal reasons, they consume cannabis because it helps them to feel better.

Unfortunately, minorities have fallen victim to the negative mentality associated with cannabis (as well as the federal legislation) more so than anyone else. Our criminal justice system has failed them, putting a disproportionate number of minorities into prison for selling or using cannabis. The statistics are alarming. Yet, this goes back to our earlier conversation about inequitable access to information because of a lower socioeconomic status. Minorities are notoriously victims of these conditions and as a result, many do not look beyond their circumstances. They become victims to a drug war.

On a deeper level, they become victims to both sides of the drug war. Many in this current generation of young Latino entrepreneurs are not taking advantage of the potential opportunities available to them in the cannabis industry. Many of them were raised by mothers, grandmothers, and aunts whose spouses and loved ones (mostly males) were put behind bars. These women raised their young children to fear interacting with cannabis. Where there was an opportunity for these women to educate, they instead instilled guilt. This is because they saw the negative results of their spouses' interactions with the plant. They did not want the same thing for their own children. Unfortunately, these kids grow up demonizing the plant and staying away from it. As a result, they miss out on opportunity in a workspace that could benefit from their insight and potentially make their own lives better.

I cannot say enough how important it is to educate yourself. Don't just regurgitate what you have been fed. With a proper education you can take whatever stance you so choose. Be a victim or be an advocate.

If cannabis were legal and not associated with a negative stigma, this situation would not occur in the first place. Remember, minorities have been stamped with the negative views of the plant since the early 1900s. They have been fighting an uphill battle ever since.

The history of cannabis interestingly contributes to this conversation. In the plant's infancy (I am talking early on, before 1910), it was referred to as cannabis—it was oftentimes used medicinally, and some of the plant extracts were even used in the medicines of large pharmaceutical companies. At this point, users were not consuming the plant by smoking it, and they did not until the influx of Mexican immigrants seeking refuge from the civil war came over. With them, so too came the practice of smoking marijuana. Cannabis quickly became part of mainstream society and as it did, it became clear that different cultures engaged with the plant in different ways. Though, regardless of culture or the methods of consumption, all people used the plant for the same reasons; either they just liked the way it made them feel, or they found some sort of relief for a health condition. Not long after this, cannabis was criminalized, and the onslaught of negative propaganda began. White Americans began to associate cannabis with their foreign counterparts (who consumed it more conspicuously), and it quickly became known as a substance that was more likely to corrupt you than it was to help you. Long story short, the negative stigma against cannabis persisted in large part because of xenophobia and racism. As I said above, minorities still pay the price for the racism and xenophobia that are inherent within our culture to this day.

This is one of the reasons that incorporating minorities into the workplace is so important to me. In a lot of ways, it allows us to take our power back. It also puts us in a place where we can use our position to help create a wave of change throughout the nation.

The word marijuana is becoming outdated. Some people in the community consider it to be derogatory. There is a lot of speculation about the origins of the word, but the consensus is that the word has foreign origins. Some people believe that it is simply a blending of the names "Maria" and "Juana," which would translate to Mary and Jane, respectively, in the English language. The word may actually have its origins in South or Central America. Some people believe that Chinese traders brought cannabis or "me ren hua" (this translates to hemp seed flower) to the Americas where the plant and its name were readily adopted. Interestingly enough, people native to Central America sometimes to refer to cannabis as "Chinese oregano." Regardless of the exact origin, one thing is for sure; the word has foreign roots and for this reason it was highly criticized. Racist politicians used it during the onslaught of their anti-cannabis tirade because they wanted to be clear that Americans knew that it was a cultural vice. As a result, the word marijuana became associated with something "bad." It's origins, like the plant itself was foreign, and the powers that be at the time were not going to let the masses forget it.

During this period, people had already been interacting with the plant. Presidents grew hemp on their farms. Americans interacted with it. But, the very minute it became associated with a different race, it became outlawed. The same stigma that started in the early 1900s continues today. Does this change your perspective on the plant? It should. This propaganda was based in fear and racism and had nothing to do with the plant itself—the plant that has therapeutic effects that cannot be ignored.

Experience is our greatest teacher. We are the greatest facilitators of our own learning. I used cannabis as an example of this, of taking learning into our own hands and avoiding the acceptance of commonplace teachings.

As I entered into the world of start-ups there was an invisible playbook that defined the ins and outs of being a founder. Had I stuck to that playbook, I would not have been successful. To be truthful, there is nothing that prepares you for the roller coaster of being a founder except for experience itself. Micro-movements based on experience begin to dictate the bigger picture. Experience translates to evidence that morphs into data along the way. Analysis of this data allows for growth and transformation. Remember this: we all have to start somewhere. As you begin to forge your own path, I urge you to forge it off empirical, experience-based data. Find your baseline and rise.

I learned quickly that experience is the only teacher. What we hear is not always the truth, and without real-world empirical evidence so much of what we are told is nothing short of hearsay. If you are curious about anything in life—conduct your own research. Don't take everything at face value.

Take Calculated Risks
calculated
/calculated/
adjective

(of an action) done with full awareness of the likely consequences

You only live once; make the most out of it. You have heard it from me and perhaps from other people too. I think it is easy to get so caught up in life, that you forget to live. I remind myself often that this life is the only chance I have to do everything I want to do. I move forward every day with this mind-set. However, with mantras such as these, it is easy to think that you should live your life however you wish and take as many risks as possible while doing it. This is not necessarily true. Not every opportunity is a once-in-a-lifetime opportunity that is going to make your life better. Some opportunities are not opportunities at all; they are curveballs that can leave you stagnant or backtracking. That said, you will be presented with many pathways on your journey. Choose them wisely.

Life is about balance. Creating success in life is about taking the right risks. There is a difference between a risk and a calculated risk. A calculated risk is choice based on empirical evidence and a logical thought process. It equates to opportunity; opportunity is the door that says, "Here is a solution you can make work." It is intelligent, calculated, and directional. You take this risk because you foresee a long-term (or even a short-term) benefit from it. A risk that is devoid of calculation is also devoid of thought. If you are going to make a decision, invest time and thought into it. Don't say yes to something because it sounds like a good idea or because it "feels right." Such a risk equates to chance—it is a gamble; a risk that can detract from an opportunity. I won't say here that an uncalculated risk will lead to failure. When you are working hard and moving forward, the process may come with "setbacks," but the only true failure is in giving up and not putting your best foot forward after you fall down. If you pick the wrong door, take what you learned from that house, and move on to the next. You have to be willing to fall and stand up only to fall again. Failure is part of the process. Embrace it.

As you make decisions you must be willing to listen to yourself. Doing this can be harder than it sounds. Science is beginning to show us that our intuition is a result of our subconscious mind doing calculations. Our subconscious mind evaluates patterns brought in through our consciousness. If something seems out of line or out of rhythm, the unconscious parts of our brains are notating this. That little voice you hear or "feel" is your brain detecting something that is outside a pattern. Really, this is for our survival. Patterns keep us alive. We depend on patterns and succession. When data stops adding up, our subconscious mind starts screaming. You need to listen to yourself when it does.

People have asked me if I am intuitive or logical—if I go off of my gut or my mind. My answer is always the same: I rely on my mind to make decisions. To me, my gut is my mind. My mind receives sensory input generated from my surroundings, whether I am aware of it or not. It is not my stomach that does this. It is my working brain, filled with neuronal connections so intricate we have yet to fully understand all of their processes. Every sensation that we have is a result of our nervous system. If I feel something in my gut, it is because of the nerves ingrained in those tissues. My choices are based on logic that is based on my mind's interpretations of my surroundings or my interactions.

Take fear for example. Fear is an emotion we feel as a result of a perceived threat. What part of our body is perceiving that threat? Our nervous system. Can we "feel" it in our stomach? Absolutely. But why do we feel it there? Because of our nervous system, a body system intricately woven to detect process and send signals through our body. Because of this, our bodies feel fear just as much as our minds, and we interpret fear because our brains detect a change in patterns. Intuition is the same thing. It is calculated in our minds and felt in our guts. What you feel is your brain doing its work.

The work done by our brains gives us the power to choose. That said, we are empowered to choose but we are not free from the consequences of our choices. This is why it is so important to listen to that voice; it means that the neurons in your brain have been hard at work. It also means that you should choose wisely and take the path that leads to opportunity. Of course, it can be hard to distinguish between the two.

A calculated risk and a risk can present themselves to you at different times in your life. Perhaps you are presented with an option for change at a time in your life where you have been casually coasting. At that time any choice could seem like an exciting one. You may meet someone who presents you with an opportunity to do what you have always wanted, and your initial reaction is to say yes and jump right in. However, there are circumstances where this is not the best plan.

It is exciting when opportunity knocks. You feel wanted and accepted, and these sentiments translate into excitement. Your serotonin starts to flow, and you grow more eager as this chemical clouds your judgment. Meanwhile, your subconscious is yelling at you that something is not right, showing you red flags that you refuse to see because you are so excited. Despite your mind telling you not to, you do it anyway.

My best advice for you to deal with this occurrence is to be honest with yourself. Opportunity can look shiny. In fact, it usually does. But allow yourself to ask the hard questions and to see what you do not want to see. The world is full of people who will tell you what you want to hear. Even more so, we tell ourselves what we want to hear for fear of having the difficult conversations that come with introspection and self-awareness. I am here to tell you what you may not want to hear. Have those conversations with yourself and with other people. Sometimes you need to have conflict in order to get what you want. Just remember, if you listen to yourself and do what serves you, you will always be on a path to greatness. Perhaps Shakespeare said this best, "To thine own self be true."

The best plan may be staying where you are until you create your own opportunity or until one that is more aligned with your vision of success crosses your path. As I was beginning my new job, I saw all of the red flags glowing right in front of me. I saw them, and I ignored them, brushing them off and figuring that everything would work out. Every red flag I saw turned out to be exactly what it looked like. I ended up leaving for the same reasons I was hesitant to come on board. Facts don't lie. What you see is not a lie. If something does not add up, or if promises are unmet, you have your answer. You have a red flag. Move on. This is an opportunity to practice honing your ability for self-propagation and to know the value of your worth. Don't settle.

When such an option crosses your path, ask yourself—will this contribute to my success? The outcome of your choice should be evidence based. The research that you conduct should help you better understand if you are stepping into a great opportunity or just rolling the dice.

In my early years, I took nearly every opportunity that was available to me, saying yes despite glaring red flags. I used to think that any job offer was an opportunity that could enhance my career. My twenty years of experience has led me to understand that this is not true. I entered into many of my start-ups, not based on logic but because it was something to do at the time. I was younger and less experienced. Doing something seemed better than doing nothing. Though ultimately, I wanted to be challenged.

My third start-up that I entered into was with a company named Kamino. I founded this company alongside two of my friends for no reason other than the opportunity to do so came across my path, and to be frank, I was bored. I had just been laid off from Mobile Roadie, and I thought, "Let's do this thing." I jumped on board because, like the rest of my prior jobs, it just so happened to come across my path. The first red flag should have been the fact that I was not remotely passionate about this project, which was centered around a very specific type of travel and tourism. Secondly, I entered into this start-up with friends. I am sure you have heard the adage about keeping your friends and your work separate. Well, this saying originated for a reason. When you are friends with the people you work with, it makes it more difficult to be candid, which in turn reduces your productivity. I ignored these two factors when I entered into the start-up and I should not have. These were problems that resulted from a quick decision devoid of deeper thought. The risk in this was failing.

Opportunity can be hard to navigate, especially as a technologist. Having the skill set to be a technologist is very much in demand. You are usually unavailable, and there is no lack of opportunity. Everyone wants or needs you. Especially in today's society. The potential for growth for someone with a background in computer science is exponential. Though, like the popular trope or popular jock or cheerleader, you need to know that you have options. You need to knock on doors and weigh the benefits and the risks of walking through them. You can take the time to do this because remember, you are part of the it-crowd. There is nearly always a place for you!

While I gained experience in each of my start-ups that ultimately contributed to my success later on, I believe that other opportunities could have come along that would have benefited me even more. This is the point I am trying to make here—there will be stepping-stones in your career, but pick the right ones. Pick the ones that will help you to become successful, the ones that you are passionate about, and the ones where you can learn. Make choices that will put you on a trajectory to success.

Remember as you are on your journey that passion is an emotion that must be balanced with practicality. You can be enamored and excited about your choice, but it should not be something that you do for the sake of experience. Choose the path that you are practically passionate about, the one that will get you closer to where you want to go and make you happy along the way. Keep in mind, that what makes me happy is not what makes you happy. We all define happiness differently, and only you can know what makes you tick.

Find a Problem and Solve It

solve

/solve/

verb

find an answer to, explanation for, or means of effectively dealing with (a problem or mystery)

Your ideas, like your children, are probably not as cute or as special as you think they are. There, I said it and not with the intention of offending you. My goal here is to insert practicality into your own individual process.

Plenty of problems already exist, whether existential, financial, or medical. Outside of personal lives, problems arise every day in various industries, old and new. You just have to be willing to find them, and sometimes you just need to be willing to look ahead. More importantly, you need to be willing to do your research.

I was in my late twenties when I came across an opportunity to work as a CTO for a company. I decided to take the position for the same reason most people cheat on their significant others. I was bored. I mean I was fucking bored out of my mind. For people who know me, they know that bored Roger is not the best version of Roger. I like to be busy, and I like to be busy doing innovative and meaningful tasks. Working as the CTO sounded fun, so I took the position.

I can't say that I was surprised when this experience turned out to be exactly what I thought it would be. For many reasons, this start-up was not successful. One of the biggest reasons was that the founder had designed a product that had little market value. Why did it have such little value? Because he created a product without first assessing whether it was something that people wanted or needed. No one needed or wanted what he had to offer, and other companies were already doing something similar. There was no niche to fill. In other words, he was trying to develop a solution for a problem that did not exist.

This is risky and, quite frankly, stupid. Too much work goes into a start-up for you to find out later that no one even wants what you created. If I could go back in time, I would have requested market research data to prove that people wanted the product. Take Snapchat for example. Was there a problem? Yes (well kind of). However silly it might sound, college students wanted a way to send naked photographs and erase the proof. Though they will never admit it publicly, Snapchat was created to allow for just this. People could send photographs that would disappear in a moment's notice from their phones, never to be seen again. For a while, people felt as though they were operating under a safety net. They sent pictures freely, knowing that they would be gone in five seconds.

This was appealing to a lot of people. People did not want evidence of what they were doing because sending a naked picture is considered to be illicit. It is not something you typically share with your family and friends; it is personal. It is something done privately for personal reasons.

When I got into the cannabis industry, it was in its infancy, transitioning from underground grows and the illicit market to legalization in specific states. The underground space was booming, and bringing it into the light required finesse. I went from sitting in meetings across from a man with a BlackBerry to sitting in meetings across from a guy who had a gun strapped to his waist. The underground space was different than the public realm of big business. The language was different. The interactions were different. We were working to liaison cannabis's journey into the public eye. Some states, such as Colorado, had an easier time with this than others.

Colorado, following suit with its liberal nature, was leading the cannabis revolution. Prior to statewide legalization, many locals were already flocking to dispensaries to get cannabis to fulfill their medical needs. Suddenly, in 2014, Denver had a population boom with people coming to the state because cannabis had been legalized. As a result of this, habitual users who had been going to the same dispensaries for years were faced with long lines. This became frustrating for them because they knew what they wanted and usually needed the plant for medical reasons. They could not afford to wait in long lines. So, many of them began turning to other dispensaries or the illicit market, sick of being held in the fixtures. This was a problem for both users and dispensaries who were beginning to lose business.

You may have noticed that I have used the term "illicit market." What I am referring to here is what is commonly referred to as the black market, the industry associated with the trading of illegal substances and firearms. The terminology, much like that of cannabis, is shifting because the term has a negative connotation that is often applied to African Americans. It is subtle racism. But have you ever stopped to think about why we called it the black market? Is it a coincidence that we call it the "black" market and then attach a negative connotation to it?

Racism is not always loud. Sometimes it is subtle and so ingrained within our culture that we do not even realize it is there unless we pay careful attention. Language is a powerful tool for shifting mind-sets. We can gloss over it and go with the status quo, or we can make a change.

The market is not black, it is illicit. The sheep is not black, it is different. Blackmail is not black, it is extortion.

Being blacklisted is banishment. We don't need to say that these things are black. We need to recognize that every time we make these statements, we are contributing to the racism embedded within the framework of our culture. We need to do better.

We did not create this problem; we found out that it existed. To come up with a solution we flew out to Colorado and interviewed several dispensaries, digging into what we could curate that would be both helpful and beneficial to them. Thus, formed the solution—we would offer consumers the ability to search for dispensaries and preorder their desired product from an online menu for purchase in the store (Legally, we could not allow for online purchase. This took, you guessed it—research). Additionally, consumers would be able to investigate the different products. We wanted to help serve people what they needed, not tell them what they needed. When they showed up at their dispensary, their order was waiting for them. No lines, no long conversations, no long waits. Just in and out. David, one of my cofounders, worked to design the front end as I worked on the back end. In other words, he worked on the aesthetics as I plugged away at the logic and data. Within five weeks we put out our prototype.

One thing all start-up founders learn is that it is better to be quick to market with a product that may be less than perfect than late to the market with a perfect product. Don't try to boil the ocean; do what you can and progress the baseline. This was especially true in the cannabis industry where nothing on the tech side even existed. Naturally, our product evolved over the years, each time offering a solution to a problem that already existed. There was no need to create an issue where there was none. There are plenty of problems that already abound not just the cannabis industry but so many others.

My advice to you, which fits into the theme of this chapter, is to do your research. Find a problem and then research it. Dive into every bit of information you can, talk to people in the industry, and find out what they did. Nothing that we created was done with blinders on. Every choice we made was analytical, calculated, and informed. To spend your time and money doing anything other than this is impractical. You will crash and burn before you even begin to get your feet off the ground.

Enhance Optionality

optionality

/optionality/

noun

the quality of being available to be chosen but not obligated

Human nature oftentimes works in curious ways. For many of us, as soon as we are told that we cannot have or do something, the more desirable it becomes. You want to do it. You need to have it. You are practically crawling out of your skin to get "it." Years of research has gone into the psychology behind this. The causes for this phenomenon aside, it is a fact. The majority of us seek out that which we feel restricted or suppressed from.

Personally, I believe that we should be offered the freedom to choose. What we can and cannot do should not be (but sometimes is) dictated by a higher power. I believe that this freedom across all aspects of life can and would elevate the level of thought from its baseline. The baseline of your thoughts should not be the bottom. Don't refer back to the lowest versions of your thoughts—seek to elevate them.

Optionality increases our potential for growth. The more you are able and allowed to do, the more you have the potential to know. The more experience you have, the more enhanced your worldview becomes. This adds potential to the level of your thoughts and ultimately your own evolution. As your thoughts rise, so too does your being. The more you know, the more decisions you can make about what you desire, what you like, and what you want. There is a power in optionality that cannot be ignored and yet we are not given options at every turn. There are rules and regulations placed upon us that dictate what we can and cannot do. Some with good reason, and others for no "real" reason at all. In a lot of ways, our system fails our humanity. It inhibits the curiosity that is inherent within the human condition. It tells us what is good for us and what is bad for us. It tells us what we can and cannot do. I think we should be able to make these choices for ourselves. This in turn enhances our worldview, our intelligence, and eventually the level of our thoughts. Imagine if this were allowed to all of us, across all sectors of life. We would be a community with the ability to intersect at the highest level of thought. There is a power in that that cannot be ignored.

There are always going to be people who do not agree with your choices. This is normal. Not everyone is privy to the same information. We all have different upbringings, and we have different perspectives and belief systems, all of which influence our choices.

As I said, we should be able to make choices. We should be able to decide where we go to school and where we work. I believe in optionality because of its correlation to potentiality, but also because I think that it is a basic human right. At the end of the day, you get only this one life. At the end of your life, will you be happy knowing that you did what you wanted to? Or you did what you were supposed to? You will not be happy if you spent your entire life doing what you think you are supposed to.

All of the choices I made were conscious. Sometimes I look back on my classmates at Duke and what they are doing. Some of them are making loads of money working for big companies. Their choices, like mine, were all conscious. I like to think that they ended up where they wanted to. I did not want to end up on that same track. I was different, and according to my professor, Dr. Astrachan, I always had been. He said that what set me apart is that he would tell us to do "x, y, and z," and I would never just accept that as the status quo. I would morph "x, y, and z." In a lot of ways, that is what I ended up doing with my career. Like my classmates, I found success, but I found it in a different way.

The power to make a choice is a basic liberty. Without the ability to make a choice we are unable to discover the truth for ourselves.

Appealing to the consumer mind-set by allowing for optionality helped to fuel our CRM platform in a lot of ways.

I often take issue with the use of acronyms in a business setting. I think they exist so that the people who use them can feel superior. That notion of superiority breeds power and a sentiment that they are on top.

I get asked often, "What does the CRM platform do?" I am always happy to explain the intricacies of what we created. Yet, I am always fascinated by how many people do not know what CRM means. They quickly pretend they know instead of just asking what it stands for.

I think this is a huge problem in our society. For fear of looking less than intelligent, we don't ask. We pretend to know and in the process, we only hurt ourselves. All asking requires is a bit of humility.

Humility is an essential characteristic for growth and success. It is OK to ask questions. It is OK not to know.

Since you asked, CRM stands for customer-relationship management. These words represent an approach that is used to facilitate a company's interactions with current and potential customers.

At Baker, we created a CRM platform that did the following:

• Gave customers the ability to intersect with a new product in a normalized way.

• Allowed consumers to see all of their options.

• Helped customers to understand what one product versus another could offer them.

• Allowed users to have what we all deserve—the liberty of choice.

Be Authentic
authentic
/authentic/
adjective

of undisputed origin; genuine

I was in my twenties, coasting at times and finding myself along the way. Prior to entering into the world of start-ups, I had spent years doing consulting work on my own. At the time, I did not feel challenged, and I was definitely in the market for a change. As I "settled in" to my role as a founder and navigated the wacky world of start-ups, I realized firsthand that being a good founder required authenticity. To me, authenticity is about advocating for your perspective, but also constantly calibrating its validity.

Having a perspective and advocating for it despite contrary facts is not just mulish, it is counterproductive and diminishes the value of your opinion.

Align with the facts, and don't kid yourself. There is no room for illusion. You can't lie to yourself, or others, about what you want, what needs to be done, and why it needs to be done. Trying to fill in the gaps of knowledge of experience by "faking it till you make it" has always been limiting advice. Knowing what you don't know, seeking to align with those who can teach you (and you, them), while preserving the skills that you personally bring to the table, can be the difference between making it, or faking it. To be authentic means that you are unapologetically you. It means having depth, long-term vision, and belief in yourself.

Like most things in life, cultivating authenticity is a process. It does not happen overnight. It happens with conviction. It happens with awareness. It does with a dedication to improved based introspection. From my experience, I have learned that the greatest founders, the greatest people, for that matter, are authentic. They are not pretending; there are no magic tricks. They are honest, humble, and dedicated to their vision. They do not apologize for what they want or what they need; they are filled with an endless desire to do better and to be better than they were the day before. Wielding these characteristics is not something that you can ignore, whether you are working beneath a founder or you are a founder yourself.

As a founder, you should be all of the things I described above. You should be personable and sincere if you want to be truly convincing. You should be so sure of yourself that you can stand behind your words and so humble that you can admit when you are wrong. I guess what I am saying is that you should be human, but the best version of human. I have had experience with many types of people, some founders, some not founders. The people I have always struggled to respect are the ones who have the mentality of "fake it till you make it." At first impression, these people seem charismatic, personable, and genuinely concerned with doing the right thing. Then, as time goes on, the mask fades, and you realize that they don't even know who they are. Don't get me wrong; there is nothing wrong with charm or charisma so long as you are also authentically you. If you are going to bring investors on, let your charm and the evidence convince them to buy into your company. Do not operate on charisma alone. Being charismatic is part of the package but it is not the whole package. I have encountered founders and coworkers who are not authentic. They play a game of make-believe for the purpose of optics. They want to appear a certain way so they carry on with a "fake it till you make it" kind of mentality. As you know, I have never liked this saying. Stop faking and start being genuine. If you cannot be genuine or real about what you are doing, move on.

So often, people fake it because they feel a pressure to know everything. They think that they need to be the so called "master of everything" in order to be a convincing and productive leader. They get so caught up in pretending to know everything that they lose sight of the potential that is practically glowing in plain sight. I am going to let you in on a secret—you do not need to be the master of everything. You just need to be you. So many folks feel the need to know more than they do, so they pretend to know. They get so caught up in pretending to be the master that they begin to lose site of the opportunity in front of them.

And as we have talked about, you are human, which means you do not know everything! And this is more than OK! The most authentic thing that you can do is admit that. You will never regret acting out of humility or being honest. So, I urge you, be humble and ask questions. Do not worry about looking stupid. It is likely that other people in the room are wondering the same exact thing that you are. There is no shame in not knowing, there is shame in pretending to know. You owe it to yourself to learn the information. Improve yourself, and more importantly, know that you can never go wrong with honesty and transparency, especially if you are running a company.

I will also say this, if you find yourself in a situation where a leader within your company (or just in life) is not authentic, it is OK to walk away. You do not need to stay where you are if you have a problem with it.

My experiences have taught me the importance of doing my homework. It is essential to know who you will be working for and with (as well as the ins and outs of the product). The other part of this is to believe the data that you have collected. Your research is not lying to you. It is data based. Give yourself the gift of self-awareness and do what is best for you based on the information that you have in front of you.

Where Work Happens

work

/work/

noun

a task or tasks to be undertaken

Sometimes the trials and tribulations of life come at you all at once. One day you are cruising down the street with the sun on your face, and the next day you are totally and completely overwhelmed.

In 2014, I found myself in the midst of so much transition that my head was spinning. I had just gotten out of a two-year relationship and consequently had to find a new place to live. This was no easy feat in a place like Brooklyn. At the same time, I had just decided to sunset my previous start-up that left me with little to write home about. I had not attained the success I wanted to, nor did I gather much of a fiscal reward. Everything that I had come to know over the years was morphing more rapidly than I could have imagined into unknown territory. The unknown included working with two other entrepreneurs, David and Joel, to start Baker. This company was the positive part of the merry-go-round that was my life during this period.

I knew that this work with David and Joel could turn into a big success. It was new and exciting. So, I decided to push forward and focus on the opportunity ahead. Consequently, I began to hunt for an apartment that would fit my budget, rationalizing that it would be best to just stay in Brooklyn. This proved to be a lot like finding the light switch in the middle of a large, pitch-black room. The longer I searched for a new place to live, the more I could not help but think that getting another apartment in Brooklyn would be a reckless allocation of financial resources. So often, the price for a dinky apartment was three to four times what you would ever expect.

I understand the prices. It is what you get when you decide to live in a city like New York. You are blocks away from culture, food, and energy. (Not to mention Brooklyn was one of the biggest hives of cultural diversity in the world.) The more I thought about this, the more I began to realize that it was not just Brooklyn that I loved, it was the parts that composed the whole that I enjoyed most. Turns out, I really just love cities. While I lived in places such as New York, Los Angeles, London, and Chicago, there was a lot of the world that I had yet to explore.

One thing that being an entrepreneur has taught me is that you should always be looking for a better alternative.

Whether you are selecting hosting providers or finding design talent or being creative with a marketing budget, there is nearly always a better option. There is more often than not something to be gained by being creative with your solutions. That being said, I decided that it was high time I got creative with my living situation and I did. I began by laying down a plan to become a digital nomad, rationalizing that I did not need to work in Brooklyn. I could work anywhere.

I started by making a list of fifty-two cities that I wanted to visit, resolving that I could work from anywhere in the world. I turned to Airbnb to find temporary homes and as I did this, I realized that it would actually be more affordable for me to spend one week in an Airbnb in a different city than it would be to lay down roots in Brooklyn.

Ultimately I made this decision for a few reasons. Yes, it was better for my budget, but it was also a chance to enhance my worldview and learn more about my country.

I wanted to be as economical as possible so I made sure that the Airbnb's that I planned to stay in had kitchens where I could cook. (I carried around my cooking utensils and made an effort to cook at "home." What host doesn't want homemade food from a guest?) I found free one-week memberships at the local gyms in each of the cities and sought to find any co-working spaces that would be willing to do the same.

With my cities and finances mapped out, I came up with a route that would start in New York. I would then head south along the coast and find my way into the Midwest before turning back south again. Instead of crossing into Mexico, I would follow the Pacific coast up toward Canada, make my way to Vancouver and then find my way to the eastern border until I hit Nova Scotia.

The day to leave came quickly. I packed my trusty Subaru and headed toward Philadelphia, my first stop. It was only ninety minutes from home but these ninety minutes proved to be a gold mine for introspection as I dug deep into my myself, mentally going through my hopes for my journey as my car rumbled against the pavement. I came to a few conclusions: I hoped that at the end I would be able to speak more intelligently about the different cities within our country and Canada. I also hoped that I would be able to build a network of friends around the world.

Once I got into a rhythm, I learned that life as a digital nomad was pretty easy. As I explored the highlights of each city, I managed to work along the way, finding either a co-working space or taking recommendations from the local city dwellers as to the best coffee shops. The cycle of new introductions and fleeting goodbyes became commonplace. It was as nerve-wracking an experience as it was exhilarating.

Like the phoenix that I had just recently tattooed on my arm (I like getting tattoos to commemorate pivotal life moments), I felt as though I was rising from the ashes, born again. New beginnings were fresh on my mind (and my skin) as I forged forward on my adventure.

As I was rising, so too was the cannabis industry. For the first time, it was making its way into the light.

As I drove, from city to city, I found myself lost in thought. I wondered what people in the more conservative states would think if I told them that I worked in the cannabis industry. I promised myself that I would remain authentic, and I vowed to always be honest about my career. I decided that my response would always be "I work in the cannabis industry." Naturally, I was worried that the people with whom I was trying to make connections would make negative assumptions about me based on the fact that I was working in the cannabis industry. To my surprise, all of the people I met on my journey were accepting of my profession and more than happy to engage in conversations about the plant and the potential for legalization.

I was startled by the overwhelmingly positive conversations I ended up having and even more amazed by the ones that I overhead. One conversation between two police officers in the seemingly conservative state of North Carolina left my eyes wide open in surprise. One of the officers was telling the other that he could not wait for cannabis to be legalized in North Carolina so that he could apply for his license. Naturally, this juxtaposition is not one that we would assume to take place. Police officers have long been required to uphold the law and arrest individuals for possession of cannabis. Yet, this particular officer was wishing that it was legal for him to consume the plant. Clearly, he was upholding a law that he did not believe in, yet, per his line of work he had no choice.

I found more so than anything that people had questions (a lot of them). They did not want to criticize the plant, they wanted to learn about it. I also learned that people were hungry for opportunity. The cannabis industry was a mecca of opportunity, and many people recognized this.

In the end, I did not make it to all fifty-two cities. Though the final city in which I ended up changed my life forever.

I was in the southeast when I got the call to come out to Colorado to be part of the first of many meetings discussing a possible acquisition of our fledgling company. I headed straight to Denver where I spent the next few years of my life building a company that I will be proud of until the day I die, a company whose initial core products were built largely in coffee shops around the United States.

Remember this: work can happen anywhere.

BE A CELEBRITY
by TIKI BARBER

Tiki Barber is renowned - as the former running back for the New York Giants, as a Broadway actor, as an author, speaker, and human being. His impact on the concept of reconciling talent with humility, especially in the professional athletic arena, has led to a powerful philanthropic vision that continues to guide his journey.

BE A CELEBRITY

celebrity

Icelebrityl

noun

someone who is celebrated for doing their job well

Celebrity. The very word has an alluring ring to it. Ask most people what I am, and they will tell you that I fall into the celebrity category. And why? Because I can command a professional football field? Because I can command a Broadway stage? Because I can author a best-selling book? In short, yes. In our world, a celebrity is famous; they hold a unique space in the eyes of society, and most people dream of becoming one.

When I was at the height of my professional football career with the New York Giants, I would often be asked to speak at schools around the area. The kids would look at me like I was some sort of God. Some of the braver ones would run up to me and tell me that they wanted to be a professional athlete too. I remember wondering why schools didn't ask for astronauts, scientists, and businesspeople to come and speak to the kids. If they did, would more kids want to run businesses? Be scientists? Would kids run all doe-eyed towards chefs and ask for their autographs? I could not help but imagine what these very kids would seek to become if their role models from a young age were people other than athletes.

Don't get me wrong, being a professional athlete is incredible, but like every job, it is not without sacrifices and challenges. The bottom line is that we need to start molding leaders who can make an impact. We need scientists. We need astronauts. We need entrepreneurs. We need to present these ideas and these other types of professionals to kids at a young age. We need them to help the next generation be aware of the world, and if we do it right, we can help ignite in them a passion for making a change. Whether or not you speak at schools or would consider yourself to be "famous" it is your responsibility to make an impact.

After I visited the schools, the kids would often write to me. One letter, in particular, stood out to me. A young girl wrote to me, and she asked, "What's it like to be a celebrity?" I rolled my answer around on my tongue. I had a lot to say, and I wanted to think of the most powerful and concise way to say it. I wrote back to her, and I asked her to think about what the word "celebrity" really means and then I told her that "celebrity" literally means to be celebrated for doing your job well. I felt like I had a chance to make an impact here, so I told her that since her teacher was a celebrity, so was the mailman and the teller at the bank. In this letter, I was able to challenge a young girl to think about the label of celebrity differently. I was able to turn the word into an equalizer, not a modifier.

If a celebrity is someone who does their job well, then, we all have the potential to be celebrities. We all have the potential to make an impact, no matter how big the spotlight or how ominous the obstacle. I am an African American male born into a low-income community. I had every opportunity to fail, and yet, my back hardly hit the ground. The fact of the matter is, I was fortunate to be born with the natural athletic ability that helped me to expand beyond the bars of my community. But more so than that, I am proud of my values and beliefs that allowed me to take my position in society and use it for good.

I know that I am lucky. I am fortunate that I was

born with the gift of athleticism because without it, I may not have had the opportunity that I did. My athletic ability provided me a way to elevate my circumstance—because of it; I was able to gain access to more opportunity in life, an opportunity not afforded to most minorities. My ability to commandeer a football field was my stepping stone, it put me on the top, and once you are on the top, you have a bird's eye view, and the entire world opens up to you. Because I was able to dominate on a football field, I was also able to become an author, an actor, and entrepreneur. And not just an author, or just an athlete, or just an actor. A best-selling author. A professional athlete. A Broadway actor. A cannabis entrepreneur.

This is not said with the intention of bragging, but I would be lying if I told you that I was not proud. I am proud. I am a man who rose from the ashes of his circumstance to become a flame. People saw me burning – I was on fire, and because of my position, I was also a leader. In this position, I felt like it was my duty to lead by example. I think so many leaders fall into the cliché of leading with love or fear. My mentality was always different than this. I did not want to be a leader for selfish reasons; I wanted to be a leader in helping make a change. I never asked myself, "How can I get more?" – I asked myself, "How can I do more?"

I want to know the many ways in which I can make

an impact, and I want to touch all the aspects of my life that will help me to leverage this. I know that by doing more, I gain respect, and I also understand that the respect I earn helps me to do more. It is a virtuous cycle.

Doing something well is a matter of working hard despite the odds or the circumstance. It is a matter of never giving up. I am proud to say that I am where I am today because I never gave up. I owe this mindset to my mom, who would tell me over and over again, "If you never stop trying you never actually fail." This always resonated with me, and it forever changed the way I thought of failure, an ominous word that holds so many people back from reaching their dreams. With my mom's words as a lighthouse, I was guided to many tiers of success. I never stopped.

I was relentless in all of my efforts because like you, I did not want to fail. But unlike most people, I never equated a mistake as a failure. My definition of failure was different; to me, failure did not exist in the conventional sense of the word. As long as I was trying to get my foot in the door somewhere, I was able to move forward. If I ever were to fail, that would mean that I had stopped trying, and that was never an option for me. It should not be for you either. It does not matter if you get fired from your job or get cut from the team. That is not failure. To fail in that situation would be to accept the defeat. To avoid failure, you must work to get a new job, one better than the one that you had before; you must be on the court or the field and put in the effort and then try out again for the team. And the best part? The show is not over until you decide to end it.

CHAPTER 4

BUILDING THE CULTURE

*What is your value? How do you measure it? What is the
point of adding value to yourself, or others? What is the
impact? In an organization, value is the beginning and
end of everything that we choose to do, and feel, and aspire
to. In my case, the principles, values, and missions that we
chose to incorporate into Baker were the differences between
our reactive expansion (which could have been brittle), and
our responsive growth (which was flexible and adaptable).
The culture of cannabis is designed to succeed because
exits are designed to keep people in industry. Amplifying
our value is a matter of transforming our ambitions into
platforms for everyone to succeed.*

***

My greatest weakness is probably that I am too hard
on people, especially myself. Consequently, I am constantly
seeking to improve and better myself. Seeking the highest
common denominator in myself comes with constant
introspection. I look within to elevate myself, squashing
the voices inside me that serve no purpose.

Though being overly self-aware can be exhausting,
I know from experience that this sort of self-awareness is
critical in order to achieve success.

Looking at our own reflection is not always easy.

In doing so, we are forced to come face-to-face with our worst enemy and greatest critic—ourselves. For some, this process of admission can be a trying one. Perhaps because we correlate our shortcomings to shame or wrongdoing. Perhaps because we have been taught to show only particular aspects of ourselves to the outside world; society teaches us to pretend to be something other than what we are. But this thought process leaves no room for human nature. We are not perfect. We will never be perfect. There is literally nothing that we can do to rid ourselves of imperfections (unless you start to border on delusional). But, what we can do is change the way we think of our imperfections. What if they were not imperfections at all, but rather, areas of improvement? What if fallibility was instead known as potentiality? I believe that if we thought along these lines we would all be more motivated to be introspective with the intent of bettering ourselves. To ignore our own fallibility seems to me a detriment to our potential for growth. Each time we ignore a fault within ourselves, we turn our backs to our own potential.

Imagine if we worked to shift this norm and instead embraced mistakes and misunderstandings from a young age. Would humility reign supreme? Would we see a marriage of ambition and humility instead of mutual exclusion of the two? I do not have a magic eight ball to tell me yes or no, but the concept is interesting.

So often we think of ambition and humility as separate entities. We think that humility equates to weakness or timid modesty and that ambition is loud and self-serving. Can they not be one in the same? Can they not be two parts that make a fortified and impenetrable whole?

In my experience, I have seen that ambition can be humble. You can be successful in loud silence. What I mean is that you do not have to scream about your success or puff out your chest in order to continue making worthy accomplishments. In fact, some of the most successful people I know are the most modest people. I think that having the self-awareness to be humble despite your success and the preceding conquest enhances your own evolution. Be so successful that your success has a voice, let the societal impact of your success speak for itself. This act, if you can manage it, becomes a testament to your personal strength and growth. It is natural to want to share your success with others, but the way in which you choose to do so speaks volumes of your character.

I recognize that this sounds easier than it is. However, I think that we also make things harder than they have to be. Choosing a union between humility and ambition is not difficult; it is different, and different, as you know does not fit the societal mold.

What is this mold, anyway? How is abiding by

norms so inherent in us that we can systematically fail to realize that individualism even exists at all? The answer is simple. Yes, there is a genetic component built into us for survival. But more so than that we are the products of our teachings. We are brought up to think, act, and speak in a particular way. And the instruction that we receive is the result of a top-down system that has already defined the qualifiers of success, of life, of our mere existence. We robotically accept these rules from the herd; we abide by them. This makes forging our own paths and curating our own definitions seem nearly impossible. That is, if separating from the herd even makes its way into our conscious thought patterns. We fall for the smoke and mirrors of society and in doing so we perpetuate expectations and with them, clichés. The end result is the status quo, which leaves little to no room for diversity and a different trajectory of growth.

We are so brainwashed by these norms that it oftentimes takes external circumstances or transcendental teachings to point out that we can make our own molds. In spite of circumstance and education, we are, and likely always will be, products of a system designed for the cliché to succeed. This leads you to think that you are less than you are. If you do not fit the shoes of the cliché, you can easily second-guess yourself and your worth. And despite your successes, you may question your accomplishments because they don't stack up to what would be considered normal. So you cower, hide, and silence yourself for fear of sounding stupid or appearing out of the ordinary. This is the stupid part, the part that we all need to recognize. It is our individualism (and the diverse community that we choose to surround ourselves with) that makes us great, not our herd.

For all intents and purposes, these negative internal notions are "symptoms" of imposter syndrome. And, to be honest, I cannot think of one successful entrepreneur who did not face this at one point in his or her career.

It is easy to avoid this mental process when you do not know enough to know what you don't know. Though, as time goes on and you garner more experience, everything that you do not know becomes glaringly obvious. You quickly realize the breadth of what you do not know. Consequently, and rather unfortunately, this period oftentimes falls around the time that a professional is rising to higher positions where they are expected to be able to handle more responsibility and more people (no better time to start doubting yourself than when you are in a management position).

I've had pangs of imposter syndrome over the course of my career for sure. For example, most recently as CTO of Baker I needed to be able to direct the efforts of a team of very talented engineers. These engineers came from a wide range of backgrounds and represented a very wide age range. As the lead technologist, I think there is an instinct to try to be everything to everybody in your organization. This is especially true when you were the person to write the first line of code.

The first time somebody asks a question you can't answer or suggests using a technology you are not familiar with is disconcerting to say the least. It feels as though you should know this. How do you not know this? You're the CTO, for Pete's sake.

Only with time and experience have I come to realize that it was my own expectations that were misplaced. I have come to realize that the role of the CTO is to support your team. You need to create trusting authentic relationships with those that you can. First, be honest with them about what you don't know, and second, entrust that they are capable of figuring it out.

So, I struggle with imposter syndrome, yes. If I weren't struggling with it, it would mean that I would have built my organization to do only things that I already know how to do, and that is not how to create success for an organization. Steve Jobs may have said it best: "It doesn't make sense to hire smart people and tell them what to do; we hire smart people so they can tell us what to do."

There is potency in this notion that should not be overlooked. Be proud of the company you keep and allow yourself to be elevated by the culture that you create. Do not let your insecurities inhibit your process. It is better to be surrounded by individuals who are a combination of highly intelligent, humble, and innovative beings.

When you think about it, it is almost funny that we doubt ourselves as we do. By nature, we are all out of the ordinary. We are all inherently unique and pretending not to be. No one knows everything. Out of concern of being more different than we already pretend not to be, we act even more according to the cliché, worried that we are not good enough. This keeps us at or below the baseline.

The cliché I continue to mention is 'privileged'. Yet, this cliché can be broken down further. What does the cliché have that allows for success to be so "easily" achieved? The cliché has:

1. Confidence
2. Access
3. Resources

It is likely that this confidence has been cultivated, perhaps through experience or perhaps as a result of environmental circumstances. The cliché likely has access and resources as a result of circumstances. Yet, how do you get access and resources if you are not the cliché? First, you need the confidence. With confidence you can begin putting yourself into situations to improve your access. (This is where it is important to think about where you want to go to school, where you want to work, and who you want to associate with.) Confidence and access together are the key that unlocks the resources.

Gaining access to the circles of success is arguably the most difficult part. This is where it is so important to run in the right circles, to say yes, and to write the dictum of your own tribe.

With all of these things, you can manufacture your own version of the cliché and elevate yourself.

Behind the confidence I created and behind the words on these pages are the conversations I did not have, conversations about my own insecurities regarding the lack of access and resources that were a result of my younger years. In the same way that I evolved to have a confident mind-set, I built a life that would give me access and resources to be successful. I built a cliché that was not a cliché at all but rather rearranged the pieces on the chessboard not just to compete but to win the game.

Success is like a game. You need certain tools to win, and you need to know how to use them while still abiding by a set of guidelines. Anybody can play the game, but you can't try to change the rules. What are these rules? They are expectations. Our system comes with expectations; it comes with things you should and should not do. These expectations can include the way we talk, the way we dress, and the circles that we run in. These expectations, these rules are defined within the system. Close your eyes. Imagine what privilege and success look like. What do they sound like? I would be willing to bet that the image you saw was similar to the one that I saw. Why? Because success, as society would define it, has a look. This exists for a reason; it is the metric that we can use to measure ourselves against. But that does not mean that we cannot take this definition and add some color to it. The rules are the standards that compose the cliché (which is a system) and (like it or not) the cliché version of success and what the people who achieve it have and "look" like exists for a reason.

The bottom line is that having resources, confidence, and access is a precursor in life to obtain success. People who want success without playing this game are taking a step too far in the wrong direction. You have to understand the game, the ethics, and why these things (access, resources, and confidence) are important. You have to frame your actions based on this understanding. Only then can you move in the right direction.

People who work in the illicit market so often ask, "Why can't I be successful in this new legal market?" The answer in response to that is pretty simple. "You are not finding success because you are not playing by the rules of the legal market. You can make it, but you need to play by the rules."

They need to know how to maneuver the system. As I said above, that is all the cliché is. It is a system, and you need to calculate your inputs based on a set of rules and standards. If you go outside that, you rarely find success because as a society we have established what it takes to succeed. This success can be cultivated. It can be acquired.

Now, imagine a working culture where the cliché is not the cliché at all, where the cliché is a group of people who played the game despite having different cards. Imagine then what you can accomplish together.

There Is Strength in Diversity
diversity
/diversity/
noun

the state of being diverse; variety

I am color-blind, but I am not blind to color. I may mix my blue with purple or my green with red. Where there is color, I see the absence of it, but I do not fail to acknowledge that hues of red and green exist. I recognize that there are people in this world, who can see what I cannot, who can know what I cannot know. But at the end of the day, this would be true regardless of whether or not my genetics had mixed the wires of my rods and cones. Even if I could see red, the same old questions would exist: "How do I know that my red is your red? How do you describe what red looks like?"

If you were to point at a plant and ask me what color it is, I would tell you that it is green because my brain knows that plants are green. Why? People tell me so. Books tell me so. That said, I see green without seeing your green. It is my green. This is my reality just so much as it is yours (regardless of whether you are color-blind or not). I cannot get away from the fact that I can't and don't see what everyone else sees. Neither can you.

One of the common tests for colorblindness is a visual test. Perhaps you already know this, but if you are being tested for color blindness, you are presented with a circular shape filled with different hues and tones of various colors. In the center of this circle, is a number. If you are not color-blind you can make out the number. I cannot make out these numbers, but that does not mean that the numbers are not there. It just means that I cannot see them. That number is only perception. Assuming you are not color-blind and I am, if we were to do this test together, our different visions are nothing more than different perceptions. We see different outputs from the same input. Is that not what life is made of? Different perceptions of the same object or being. Yet, we fight about it and we run from it. Instead of rationalizing that all we see is a perception, light absorbing and bouncing, illuminating and darkening, we argue or we walk away. Why? Because we see a difference and differences are perceived as dangerous.

Beneath what we see, there is and can be so much more so long as we allow ourselves to be open to this fact. We don't need the same languages; we just need the same visions.

If anything, my color blindness has led me to have a strong appreciation of tonality. This was a skill that I honed at Duke when I studied visual design. At first, I would design webpages in black, white, and gray, playing with the different spectrums of each of these tones. Staring at the page I thought often about how I wanted the page to feel. For a guy who is not often guided by emotion, this was an interesting and powerful part of my process. I knew that certain hues could give way to specific emotions and that emotions could influence user engagement with the site. Obviously, the goal is for the viewer to have a positive experience. I mean at the end of the day the content on a website is the content on a website. Regardless of the color, it looks a certain way. It says certain things. These things are on the page regardless of whether or not there is color. The color is a kind of a frosting. Yet, that frosting can make all the difference. Should it? What do you think?

When you think about color, it just is what it is. Primary colors, much like prime numbers cannot be broken down any further. They are what they are.

Color is not a qualifier for value, and yet we see it as so. I speak not just to webpages and billboards here but to people. Color is the surface, but the judgment you make based on the color that you see is merely your perception.

Your perception is not a reflection of reality.

Regardless of what we can see, we cannot ignore the existence of one particular thing nor can we ignore our differences. It is pointless and destructive to turn a blind eye to that which exists in front of us. True blindness inhibits growth.

I am Hispanic. I was raised to know a particular set of cultural values and yet, I allowed myself to be open to other cultural values.

We are so caught up in being politically correct, that we turn a blind eye to the strength that exists as a result of our diversity. We do not want to offend or make someone of a different culture or color feel less than so we pretend that their color and their culture don't exist at all. Doing this is the true offense. In doing this we are forcing ourselves to be color-blind. In ignoring our differences, we miss out on interactions that would potentially facilitate our growth. These differences add depth.

We are different. We are supposed to be different. Our differences keep us alive. I mean this. The diversity inherent within our DNA prevents us from all being wiped out from the same disease. It protects our species. Instead of allowing our differences to hide, we must allow ourselves to recognize and address the differences in others. I have seen over and over again how strong we can become together.

Let's say you are looking to build a company. What qualities are you looking for in people whom you want to add to it? I'm sure the basic things such as knowledge, honesty, and a strong work ethic make that list. But, what about adding color by adding diversity? To me, this is more important than adding knowledge.

Diversity is not the primary goal of my hiring process—it just so happens that a diverse group of people make for a stronger team. It will raise our potential together. My equalizer has nothing to do with the qualifiers of diversity. It has to do with the merits people bring with them.

I remember when we were building Baker, I was thinking critically about who we needed to add. We realized pretty quickly that we needed a woman on staff (and in a leadership position). Cannabis was a male-dominated industry, and I knew we needed a female on board to help us to elevate our thinking and our brand.

Diversity of people, is diversity of ideas.

We hired Carter Davidson, and we were off to the races. She was our first female hire and arguably one of the most pivotal ones. Being a female meant that Carter could bring something to the table that neither Joel, David, nor myself could bring.

Beyond that, Carter was not just a female, she had qualifiers that set her apart from the rest of the candidates, qualifiers that would add diversity to Baker. We embraced this, and we ended up thriving in large part because of it.

Since her inception with Baker, Carter has built the sales organization into one of the most successful sales organizations in cannabis. We truly would not be here without her.

To be honest, I'm not sure how Carter came to find us (look at me admitting to what I don't know) but she applied for a position as head of sales. Her background was at Salesforce which was an immediate win in my mind because she had already been through what we were hoping to achieve. We know that her background and expertise would boost our credibility, and we knew that she would be a vector to help us create a sales organization that could take us to the heights that we wanted to reach. And she did. In a lot of ways, she helped us to go above and beyond. It was a bonus that she was a female but the qualifiers that set her apart as a result of experiences (yes, as a female but also in life) were what truly elevated us.

You never know where the key to your success is hiding. Don't allow yourself to be so blinded by a cliché that you miss the gems hiding in the rubble.

Add to the Culture

culture

/culture/

noun

the customs, arts, social institutions, and achievements of a particular nation, people, or other social group

In the early days, before human resources told me I couldn't use this language anymore, I had one hard and fast rule for whom we could hire and whom we could not. Our hiring manager knew this was my one rule and would constantly echo it back to me. NO ASSHOLES!

All of my years in tech have allowed me to see every stereotype of employee that you can think of. The most toxic in my mind are the so-called "genius assholes." These are people whose skills are so incredible that many hiring managers will hire them despite some…um…character flaws. I had encountered these folks for years and I knew that they were a risk to the integrity of company culture.

I would loudly and often make this dictum to the

team. No assholes! If you weren't an asshole, you had a shot.

As you build your culture, it is imperative that you keep the assholes out. It is also important not to turn a blind eye to diversity. Here, I want to talk with you about how to build and elevate your company culture as a result of that mind-set.

If you were to ask any of my cofounders, they would probably tell you that I was the champion of culture. In a lot of ways, I was. I was constantly looking to hire people who would elevate the culture of our company. My mentality regarding this did not come from the fact that I consider myself to be ethnically ambiguous, but rather that I was ten years older than my cofounders. As a result of my age, I have seen many bad workplaces. So, building a strong and ideal workspace was important to me.

Even David, one of cofounders, will tell you that my Hispanic roots were not obvious nor were they at the forefront of my mind as we built this. Yet, he will tell you how important building this culture was to me. David had a diverse upbringing. He lived in many places around the world and found homes in regions such as Portugal and South Africa. As a result, he was nearly as diversity blind as I was. Though, like me, he was not blind at all.

At Baker, we had core values. These values came from the culture that we had created. We embodied them before we even wrote them down.

Bring a positive mental attitude.

Assume positive intent and stay in the present.

Be proactive; provide a solution.

Be curious and listen to others.

Be respectful, kind, and have fun.

Hold ourselves accountable; communicate ownership and next steps.

Embrace conflict; disagree, then commit and communicate.

Celebrate success and stay hungry.

Work with pride; keep Baker in Baker.

When Joel, David, and I began our early discussions regarding the conception of Baker we did not think, "We have the South African, the privileged white guy, and the 'ethnically ambiguous' Hispanic." But when things really got rolling, building our culture and our core values was at the forefront of our growth.

As a result of our different circumstances, you could almost say that we were elevated from the start. The compatibility that existed despite our differences helped to turn Baker into what it is today.

The wacky world of start-ups comes with unexpected twists and turns. Sometimes, all you can do is stop the bleeding. Joel, David, and I were all solution-oriented individuals, and when the going got tough we had no problems putting our minds together. The rest of our team did not either. Like I said, we were lucky. We were lucky to have the team that we did and we were successful as a result of it.

Our mentality for building a company culture was different than most. When we sought to add members to our team, we looked for a culture add instead of a culture fit. Culture fit sounds good on the surface, but if you think about it, it means that you want to hire a lot of people like yourself. It means that nothing is being added to the equation, just fit into a space to maintain the status quo. In my experience, this leads to a toxic workspace. I have seen many filled with privileged men and I have seen the stagnancy that results from it.

As we looked to build our culture at Baker, I would ask questions about people we sought to hire. "Do I want to continue to know this person better?" Meaning, would I want to sit down for a beer with this person? "Can we get along amicably and professionally?" I would also ask, "What else are they bringing to the table that we don't already have?"

I am not necessarily talking about this from a racial, gender, or cultural standpoint. For me, it was more about what they could do differently as a function of their hobbies or skill set. If their skill or hobby or perspective was different, it was an add. A culture add. Culture adds are invaluable because you bring someone into your culture who does what no one else does. This only makes you stronger. Remember, there is an undeniable potency in our differences. I have seen it over and over again in the workspace.

When I think about this, I always go back to a few examples from science. At the risk of sounding provocative, it is one of the best ways that I think I can get this point across.

In some cultures and countries, inbreeding is not necessarily frowned upon. In others it is. Have you ever wondered where this negative stigma comes from? Well, the questionable viewpoints toward inbreeding are rooted within the field of genetics.

Within our DNA, we have many genes (enough to fill up a very large book). Some of those genes are dominant and some are recessive. Dominant genes sound like their name; they are dominant over recessive genes and overall more likely to be seen within our population. For a quick example, how many people can you think of with red hair? Brown hair? You were probably able to think of more people with brown hair. Why? The gene responsible for brown hair is dominant over the gene that codes for red hair, meaning that if an individual has both of those genes inherent within their DNA, the gene for brown hair will be expressed over that of the gene for red hair. As a result, you see more people with brown hair in the population. In fact, it is expected that one day the gene for red hair may stop appearing within our population entirely.

When we mate outside of our family, and consequently our gene pool, we are not only diversifying the gene pool (which is extraordinarily beneficial for our survival) we are helping to protect ourselves from developing a genetic disease or anomaly that results from inbreeding.

When offspring is conceived out of inbreeding, their genetics can be "faulty" because the recessive traits that have been hiding in mom and dad can oftentimes be made visible since there are two recessive traits being expressed (one from mom and one from dad).

Take this example: Eastern Pennsylvania is home to beautiful farmlands and a strong Amish culture. Their population is closed, meaning that mating occurs within the boundaries of their population, not outside of it. The origins of their populations has its roots in a small number of German Immigrants (about two hundred). This group of immigrants just so happened to come to America carrying genes for some pretty rare inherited disorders, including some types of dwarfism. One form of dwarfism (found within the founders of this population), Ellis-van Creveld syndrome, leads to polydactyly (extra fingers or toes), a hole in the upper chambers of the heart, and a shorter stature. As a result of this, individuals within this population today have alarming rates of this form of dwarfism (and other rare genetic diseases).

If the men and women in this population were to step outside of their boundaries, you would see fewer and fewer cases of this rare type of dwarfism. However, because they stay and mate inside the confines of their culture, many incidences of dwarfism and other rare genetic disease increase. Why? Because inbreeding allows for recessive diseases to show up in a population. (Remember, the offspring are getting two copies of these genes so they get expressed.)

My point in this science lesson is to help you to understand that inbreeding in the work space, like inbreeding in the true sense of the word, can cause a lot of problems that otherwise would not exist. Going outside of your gene pool frequently does quite the opposite. It diversifies the gene pool, making it stronger and adds to the potential of elevating your company and your brand.

Be Symbiotic

symbiotic

/symbiotic/

adjective

denoting a mutually beneficial relationship between different people or groups

Growth potential is mutually inclusive. When founders look for new hires they are seeing growth potential in the candidates just as much as the candidates are seeing growth potential in the founders and the brands. It is rare that one would exist without the other. This is really pretty special when you think about it. This synergistic mind-set presents you with an opportunity to help each other to expand upon both of your horizons, and to go higher.

For example, our in-house counsel, Emily Gordon, had never before filled an in-house counsel role. I pushed for her to be hired, and today she has "I took the company public" on her resume. Likewise, my cofounders and I have "Our company went public" on our resumes. All of this success is a result of the symbiosis that we manufactured.

When you are starting a company, you usually don't have boundless amounts of cash. You need to be smart, and you need to find ways to bring in the best kinds of people for less money than they would normally accept.

This may seem difficult, but there are ways to compensate one another without it being financial.

One of the best ways is to offer potential hires opportunities that they will not find anywhere else, opportunities that will ultimately allow them to find more opportunity in the future.

This mind-set and this symbiosis worked for my cofounders and me just as much as it worked for Emily. I would like to think that it is something that could work for you too. When you think about it, most business-minded people are looking for the potential to grow.

Obtaining positions, especially those that would be considered higher up, is not always easy. Finding opportunities to expand upon your skill set and your resume is not necessarily as simple as it seems. So, to give someone an opportunity to do this, while building your brand at the same time is invaluable.

Enhance Your Breadth of Knowledge
knowledge
|knowledge|
noun

facts, information, and skills acquired by a person through experience or education; the theoretical or practical understanding of a subject

In start-ups (and life, for that matter) it is better to know enough about a lot, than it is to know a lot about a little. What I am trying to get at here, is similar to the point I have been trying to make throughout this chapter. When you are building your company culture, seek to elevate your culture by adding individuals with a greater breadth of knowledge.

Don't get me wrong, having a depth of knowledge on the level of a subject matter expert can be wonderful. However, one thing I have learned is that you should always seek to expand your knowledge base, no matter if you are a subject matter expert or a novice in the particular field you have entered.

Having a depth of knowledge about a wide variety of topics is invaluable. However, this is rare. It is far more common that someone will have a decent amount of knowledge on many topics than a deep amount of knowledge on many topics.

In business (and life), it is important to be able to speak to a wide variety of topics. Yes, it makes you more marketable, but it also makes the company that you work for stronger. Remember, the more you know, the more likely you are to be different, and the more likely you are to bring something to the table.

In a lot of ways, my breadth of knowledge is a function of my experiences and the conscious ways in which I sought to enhance my worldview. Trips to Costa Rica, immersion programs, Duke, my travels—they all helped me to expand my knowledge base. Right now, if pressed, I could program in about twenty-five languages. I can talk to anyone about technology on the market. I also can fix a leaky faucet and install your new light fixture. I can talk to you about literature and speak to you in Spanish. And I can make a braised short rib that will change your life. The point I am trying to make here is that I know how to do a lot of things. All of the above are exemplary.

Having a wide breadth of knowledge is a lot like having a multipurpose tool in your toolbox. You never know when you are going to need it, and when you have it, your insight can be critically valuable in many different situations.

As a CTO, you must have a wide breadth of knowledge. Before you even begin to code, you take on a myriad of roles that have nothing to do with punching away at keys on your computer.

As somebody who has been in a senior technologist role for a long time I understand that to most people what I do is a complete mystery. I know that most people understand that as CTO I'm responsible for the "technology" solutions, but few people truly understand what that entails. I suppose this isn't too dissimilar from the position of an executive chef. People know that being a chef involves cooking, but beyond that I feel like most people really don't know much about the breakdown of a professional kitchen, not to mention how the size of said kitchen impacts the responsibilities of each of its inhabitants.

The role of a CTO at a large corporate entity looks different than the role of a CTO in a start-up organization.

For example, let's take a look at the role of CTO at a large corporate entity. In that position this executive is in charge of all things tech and IT, but the role is largely focused on resource allocation. The CTO of a company that employs hundreds if not thousands of people will be much more concerned about what percentage of the company's costs are derived from engineer salary than the technical details of implementing a specific feature of the company's app. This CTO would likely have many different technical department heads reporting to him or her who would be more concerned with the minutiae of their own departments. Depending on the size of the organization even these department heads might not be that informed about day-to-day developments.

Conversely, when we look at the CTO of a start-up organization, you are much more likely to find somebody who can tell you about every line of code in the organization's codebase. More than likely that CTO wrote most of the code. If you were to ask this CTO about something such as salary or hardware expenses he or she would more than likely point you to the CEO or COO. You see, in the early stages of a company, the CTO is barely more than a glorified developer. With the financial restrictions that come with building a start-up, it would be fiscally irresponsible to hire a CTO who is not actively contributing to the code.

As I said above, in many if not most start-ups, the early CTO or "technical founder" has to do it all.

In the early days of Baker some of my tasks included but were not limited to:

• Debating whether we wanted to build a native application versus a web app
• Selecting what tools (languages) we were going to use to build our solution
• Selecting the data storage mechanism that we were going to leverage to store our data
• Selecting a hosting provider that would be low cost enough to give us as much runway as possible all while keeping in mind we would most likely need to migrate later
• Designing the structure of our databases so that we would not be at a disadvantage when it came time to scale our operation
• Selecting how we were going to manage version controlling of our code

Keep in mind that this all had to happen before I wrote a single line of code. Once all of those decisions were made, I was then the only technical resource and therefore was responsible for building everything. (To be fair, David knew enough HTML/CSS to come in handy when it came time to build our proof of concept.) Let's not forget that at the time, I'm not only playing the role of CTO, but also co-founder. (You can say my breadth of knowledge came in handy here as well.)

As a cofounder, I had to be able to communicate to my partners, who were not technical, why I was making the decisions I was. They had placed their trust in me to make the best decisions on technology (with the few resources that we had). In turn, I needed to be able to explain to them what was happening on my end. To do this, I found that it was best to contextualize and simplify concepts that were otherwise overly technical. I knew that if we were going to be successful, I was going to have to find a way to package what I knew in a way that they could understand. Distilling complex concepts is an art, and I was fortunate to learn from one of the best, Dr. Astrachan. As you can discern by now, he influenced my journey in many ways but one of the greatest lessons I ever learned from him was the art of simplification—there is no need to overcomplicate what is overly complicated. Instead, break it down, and present its parts (the parts that people will understand). While I am not sure that I am quite on his level, I think I manage to do a pretty good job.

This is one of the most important aspects of a good CTO in my opinion. A good CTO needs to be able to distill complicated technological concepts and communicate them effectively to nontechnical people so that they understand well enough what we are all deciding on. I feel that this set of soft skills is what takes somebody who might be a very good engineer and put him or her on track to be an engineering manager and potentially a CTO someday.

I tell you this to help you better understand where I am coming from. When I tell you a breadth of knowledge is important, it comes from my twenty-plus years of experience. Whether you are a CTO or a CEO or somewhere below or in between, you will benefit from knowing more about a lot of things.

Cultivate Humility

humility

/humility/

noun

a modest or low view of one's own importance;

humbleness

When we talk about building a company culture, I cannot help but speak again to humility. Humility, in my humble opinion, can be cultivated.

Too often, we get caught up in needing to know everything. Then, when we don't know everything, we panic, and we lie. We do not admit to not knowing, instead we pretend to know at a detriment to ourselves and the people around us. This is something I see all the time. Perhaps you do as well.

When you build your company, seek the humble candidates. The ones who impress you in an interview not just with their intelligence but with their willingness to say, "I am not quite sure. But I would like to learn. Can you tell me more about that?"

That is something that I want in the people I work with and also something I seek to uphold within myself. I know that I can help teach people how to write a piece of code. I am not breeding intelligence by doing this. Instead, as a result of their humility and their willingness to ask for help I am assisting them to build upon a skill set, which in turn makes our company stronger. I am helping them to increase this knowledge base.

I think back sometimes to young Roger in interviews. I can think back to one specifically where (at my friends' urging) I ended up doing just enough research to speak to a specific hot technical topic at that time. The interviewer must have known that I had no idea what I was talking about. In retrospect, this made me look less appealing because he probably thought that I was full of shit.

That being said, if you don't know, just say that you don't know. We are habituated to pretend that we know more than we do. Which is ironic because oftentimes, we are better off pretending to know less than we do. In an attempt not to look stupid, we panic and we pretend, spewing out incorrect and loosely researched content. As a result, we appear disingenuous and rather foolish.

To elevate ourselves, we need to be willing to sound "stupid" and to say that we do not know. It is OK to not know the answer. I think on a larger scale we need to shift how we define "stupid." We associate stupidity with not knowing an answer. Instead, why can't we look at not knowing as curiosity or as a potential opportunity to share information and gain knowledge?

What is curiosity? Curiosity is not stupidity. Curiosity is wonder, a desire to gain knowledge and understand something. Curiosity is bravely asking questions about the world around you, despite what you think others may ascertain. It is the ability to put your ego aside and say, I am genuinely curious.

From experience, I can tell you this—it is better to be curious in a room of people than it is to be silent. Your curiosity may lead to innovation, or it may fuel a better culture that will only improve the success of your company.

Most people have a misconception that there is a bare minimum to be in the room. They think that you need x amount of knowledge to even be at the table. They think, "Why am I here? I am not on the same level as these other people because I do not meet the bare minimum (that they all have or that I think they have)."

This lack of confidence stems from nothing more than insecure thoughts leading people to believe that they are minimally qualified. I see this a lot in young employees who are just happy to be there. They stay quiet because of this and because they know that they have less experience than the other people in the room. As a result, they stay silent, feigning understanding and hiding their curiosity. Unfortunately, this thought process has quite the opposite effect of what people intend. It keeps them at the bottom.

There is an inherent and self-inflicted expectation that you have to bring something to the table. However, the reality is that there is no minimum requirement. You can sit at the table and add to the conversation by simply asking questions. If you do find yourself at such a table, take advantage of the situation and leverage whatever you can.

It is disarming to say, "I don't know." Get comfortable saying it and learn everything that you can. And if you think that you are the most intelligent person in the room, take a hint from Confucius who once said, "If you are the smartest person in the room, then you are in the wrong room."

I will be the first to tell you that I am wrong or that I do not understand. (Though saying that I am wrong is not always easy.)

This may come as a surprise to you that even my admission of wrongdoing is calculated. In my personal relationships (e.g., parents, siblings, significant others), even when I know that I am wrong, I have to go through the internal process of preparing to admit it. Not because I don't want to but because it is hard to squash my internal ego if I have calculated that the person to whom I have been wrong did not have the answer either.

In my head, I have a chart and this chart is filled with what I think certain people know on specific topics. In other words, I have expectations that some people will know more or less about specific topics than I do. When my calculation does not equate to reality and I find myself wrong at the hands of someone "lower" on my chart, it is even harder for me to admit to being wrong. Now I want to be clear here. When I say "lower", I am not talking about intelligence. I am talking about perceived experience. As you may have gathered, I am proud of my breadth of knowledge and my ability to discuss a variety of topics. I have gathered a wide range of knowledge just for this reason. So, when I find myself wrong at the hands of someone I did not think had the same shared experience as me, it surprises me and takes me a moment to admit to being wrong.

Yet, I do it anyway (while trying to unclench my teeth). In my mind, I tell myself it is time to eat crow. I dig deep, and I mutter the words, "I am wrong." And you know what? Nothing bad happens afterward. Oftentimes, the conflict (if there was one) resolves itself. I adjust the calculations in my head, and I move on vowing to myself to do whatever it takes to not be wrong again.

It's funny to me that I go through this process in personal relationships but not in the workspace. In the workspace, I have no problem admitting that I am wrong. When it comes to work, ego is the enemy. By admitting wrongdoing, I create trust in the organization, and then the company moves forward. It seems backward but it works. In the long run, being wrong has helped.

Regardless of being right or wrong, having the humility to say that you are wrong will create a better work environment.

At the end of the day, this not only helps make the people around me more comfortable, it also helps me to learn. Furthermore, it opens up the door for the person across from me to be vulnerable and to be modest and to ask questions. Humility creates a safe space where growth can happen through a series of chain reactions. We feel comfortable if the people around us are willing to be vulnerable themselves.

I also know that if I want to elevate myself, I need to enmesh myself in a strong, diversified environment. I need to have a culture around me that allows me to tune into untapped parts of myself. That being said, I want a culture around me that is filled with people who are different than me. Who know what I don't know.

I am not going to lie to you here. It can be nerve-wracking to be surrounded by new people who are different than you. Yet, what we do not talk about are the insecure thoughts that we silence. Do we not all have the same introspective (and sometimes insecure) thoughts? "I should have worn this instead of that. Make sure your handshake is strong. Say this, not that. Sit up straight; you look like a hunchback. I wonder what he is thinking of me. What am I doing here? Am I qualified to be here?" These universal questions come on a rollercoaster of rushed thoughts, and what do we do instead of speaking these thoughts? We reach out our hand and we say hello. Hello. The smallest, most digestible word in all of language.

These thoughts are so often silent, these questions shoved down as we force ourselves to elevate courageously above our fears and insecurities. When you hear me say, "Hi, I am Roger," there are a million other things I could say but I choose to squash them and stand taller despite their presence. This very act is the highest common denominator in action. It is a choice to elevate yourself in spite of your self-doubts.

CHAMPION DIVERSITY
by EMILY PAXHIA

Emily Paxhia is the co-founder and managing partner of Poseidon Asset Management, guiding, stewarding, and helping build the cannabis industry. By leveraging her network, Emily has funded some of the most prominent companies in cannabis, but does so with her stringent belief that without diversity, solutions cannot exist. Her values have imprinted the way that the industry operates, grows, and empowers.

Be a champion of diversity
diversity
/diversity/
noun

the state of being diverse; variety

Where is your female?

Where is your diversity?

Where is their voice?

Who is speaking instead?

We need voices from all walks of life. We need the

perspective of a person that is not the "race, class, gender" of a typical leader.

In my effort to be a feminist - but not a separatist – I tell men that I recognize you for your efforts, but growth is about digging into fine lines and nuances.

Sometimes, the talking heads are not the best representations. Sometimes, the voices on the sidelines need a megaphone.

These voices need to be loud.

My responsibility is to listen. First, I had to listen to the experiences I had in life and those that brought me to the plant. My relationship with cannabis started after both of my parents lost their lives to the ruthless disease that is cancer. I watched my parents suffer at the hands of the disease, and the treatments designed to treat it. They were crippled by both. But, what I also witnessed was the power of cannabis. Cannabis offered my parents relief when nothing else could; all this while the world has been turning their backs on a plant that offers a premier degree of palliative care. It was and continues to be, a massive misalignment of ethics that our government created a racist, un-empowering, and disproportionate system.

What I know is this – we have destroyed ourselves with propaganda. We have failed to question the world around us. We have accepted the status quo and most of us have gone on to live the lives that society expects us to

– we are puppets to regulations and the people who make them.

The anti-drug propaganda that revolves around our nation has brainwashed us into thinking that cannabis is harmful.

To paint it badly, they used color as a weapon. And so, our society shut the door on the potential of the plant while opening prisons to house generations of people who broke arbitrary laws.

Cannabis is no gateway drug. The only gateway that cannabis opens is one that creates an equitable field of health, of innovation, and of society. Seeing the benefit that cannabis offered my parents washed away any potential that the stigma propagated by the government was true.

I rationalized that if generally "good" and law-abiding citizens would go out of their way to purchase the plant on the illicit market, it certainly had potential in the legal market. Allowing this plant some time in a legal spotlight would also allow more people to interact with it. People who had walked away because they had gotten a contaminated product on the illicit market could one day try a regulated product and get a true feel for the effects and benefits of the plant. I knew that legalization could be revolutionary. I knew that this risk was a goldmine of opportunity. I saw that opportunity in early 2014 and saw investing in cannabis as an opportunity to overturn this stigma.

To be an investor in the cannabis industry (especially in the earlier days) you need a degree of resiliency (much like the founders did) and an understanding of the intimacy of the rapidly evolving space. Our fund focused on those things, along with a nurturing and understanding mindset. My Masters in psychology comes into play often in investment, because investing is all about understanding peoples' psyches, and how to manage them, and what gets us through the arduous process of building a business, a team, and an ideology.

When Roger and I first met, one of the first questions I asked him was, "Who is on your team?" He was confident in his answer - "A pretty diverse group." "How do you interact with the plant?" He looked at me quizzically, as though he had never heard such a question before. One of the things in investing that is so important is knowing the team, and understanding who they are and their ability to navigate the choppy waters of startup worlds - in cannabis, that water is even more difficult to navigate.

Like Roger, I am a pioneer of diversity. I believe that workplaces should be filled with persons of different genders, skin colors, cultures, and backgrounds. Assimilation is limiting – by conforming to our own, we bind ourselves and our potential in chains.

Cannabis can break down barriers in the industry and around the world. And that question embodied that.

With Roger and his team, it was about the fact that they were applying the knowledge that they had from other experiences and applying them to an industry that was underserved, and I thought that was very unique. The industry has not been able to attract a great deal of people who have experience in complementary sectors, because there is so much stigma around it. When I met Roger, his experience in building tech for early-stage companies was a critical qualifier, but despite that, he had taken an interest in participating in this space.

Roger came in with the depth of experience and was interesting also because ostensibly had more to lose than younger founders who had no prior career. He had more to risk - the career and reputation.

Putting himself into a position of being a calculated risk-taker was appealing because just like me, he found opportunity in his optionality.

He brought diversity to a homogeneous space, and with it, he helped change the color that had maligned the plant for generations.

So, I continue to ask - where is your color? Of experience, of creed, of vision.

Every business in this industry needs to have a voice in shaping public opinion. Legalizing cannabis, from a criminal justice reform position is extremely important, and ensuring that the right voices are heard, we must speak up.

CHAPTER 5

BOTTOM LINE

Games don't interest me. Challenges do. To earn success, you must be willing to humble yourself and strategize your path. Destiny is earned, and planned for. You have to focus on the pieces, the moves, the ideas that progress your path, and then act on them. I was mindful of who and what would challenge me to level up, because it was the only metric of success that I could quantify. Passion, drive, focus, and pragmatism – these are the drivers of success that live to serve a vision. Visions, it turns out, are better realized when they are shared with others. The challenge is how well we can rise together.

***

Have you played Othello? It is a two-player game on an 8 x 8 grid that looks like a chessboard. There are sixty-four discs that can be played and moved throughout this board. One side of the disc is black and the reverse side is white. One player is assigned the color black. The other player is assigned the color white. The game begins with two black discs and two white discs at the center of the board; the white pieces are arranged diagonally from one another and the black pieces are arranged diagonally from one another. Each player takes turns placing his or her respective pieces. The goal of the game is to have the majority of your colored discs on the board at the end of the game. How does this work? Well, let's say you say have the white discs, and I have the black discs. If I strategically place my black discs to surround your white discs, then you flip your white disc to black. The more this happens, the closer I get to winning. Now, you have to know that it is a process and along the way you have to prepare to be set back by your opponent's moves (some of which you cannot control). Yet, in order to win, you have to keep moving forward, and you have to think about all of the potential outcomes of your choices. And, you have to keep strategizing despite the outcome in order to be successful. In life, finding your path to success is a lot like this; it requires a series of steps and setbacks with a winning (and calculated) mind-set that helps to create the outcome that you desire.

Success drives me; it always has. Opportunity steers my direction. Choices propel me to my end goal. Passions keep me in motion. Why? Because I am not someone who is comfortable with the stagnancy of the status quo. Because I do not feel entitled to anything. Anything I want, I work for, and in order to get where I want to go, I like to use careful and thoughtful introspection to move forward. Like a piece in Othello, every move is strategically planned with an end goal of being better than I was before.

That being said, I did not want my exit at Baker to

be a closed door. I wanted it to be an open one that would allow me to move forward into new experiences with the ability to accomplish more. What I saw in an exit, was not an end. What I saw was an open field of boundless, never-before-experienced access to opportunity. Maybe this is just my growth mind-set, but my bottom line was that I wanted to accomplish more. This exit was a ticket to a new and enhanced beginning. I refused to let it be anything else.

Maybe this is because I think about success differently than other people. Maybe if I thought of success as a dollar sign, an exit would be an end. However, I just can't allow myself to see it that way. I never started Baker with a deadline for getting out—but it was unrealistic to think that I could do it forever.

I get into something because of its potentiality. As I am sure you have figured out by now, I am an entrepreneur at heart and I cannot help but flow with opportunity, constantly seeking the potential for growth. The concept of doing something solely for financial gain does not resonate with me. I am someone who throws my entire self into my work experience; I dissect everything that I can from it and I allow myself to gain from anything that allows me to grow. I thrive off this. Why? Because we can grow from nearly every encounter, whether we are conscious about it or not. Subconsciously our brain makes calculations, microprocesses determine our inputs without our active awareness. What I mean is, we are subconsciously influenced by more interactions than we realize. On the other hand, there is conscious growth. This is the growth that we seek, the growth that results from actively putting ourselves into positions to mature, improve, and elevate. Conscious growth has exponential potential; it means that you are seeking to be a sponge and allowing yourself to be aware of the potential in even the smallest of interactions. I have learned to consciously take everything I can from every experience. The good, the bad, the mediocre—there is always something for me to acquire. There is for you too, whether you look for it or not.

So, while success was always something that I wanted, the exit was never my goal. If I saw continued opportunities for growth within the same company, I would not feel a strong desire to walk away from that company. As I said, I am driven by success, which to me means finding opportunity. And, opportunity comes in different shapes and sizes. And, sometimes realizing opportunity is a matter of taking what you know, holding it in your hands, and examining it from a different angle. Take the very concept of an exit for example. For many founders, the exit is considered to be the alluring pinnacle of their career. It is this supposed tantamount experience, this end all be all, where you finally get to harvest the tangible reward of your relentless efforts. But, what if we looked at it differently? What if we saw an exit as a key to more opportunity (as I alluded to above)?

An exit is the climax, not for your totality but for a particular experience. It is the height that you reach for a moment in time. Yes, if you conceive of a proper exit, you do get to reap the fiscal reward. And, I understand that the prospect of financial gain after years of falling in order to rise only to fall again and stand up once more is alluring. But, in order to be truly successful, you must be driven by something more, something deeper. After all, the desire to rise after falling is not superficial; it comes from something deep inside.

Anyone who has been a founder or worked through the early stages of start-ups knows that it requires a certain degree of fortitude, a willingness to fail, and the gusto to rise to the challenge. Without the drive, the calculations, and the proper mind-set, your climax may be a tiny hill, not the mountain you were hoping for.

Challenge yourself to look at an exit as more than an "end" to something. If you allow yourself to think deeply about this and see beyond the dollar signs, I believe that you will see an exit as a bridge to a new beginning. I think that most people see an exit as an ending (and I can see why). By its very definition, an exit means that you are getting out of something; you are departing from it. Yet, it does not have to mean an ending, unless of course, that is your definition of success. It can mean the start to something new. And it did for me, because I wanted it to.

Know Your Value

value

/value/

noun

the regard that something is held to deserve; the importance, worth, or usefulness of something

No matter our passion, our practice, or our prerogative, we all have an inherent set of values. Some of us are loyal and dependable, others are consistent and efficient. Most of us have managed to accumulate a combination of many different values. We obtain these values from our tribe, and over time as we evolve, our value sets often grow with us. We shed some (the ones that are not serving us), and we gain others (the ones that help us to level up). If we are smart, we leverage our values to elevate ourselves.

To know what our values are, we must have an intimate understanding of the self. Self-awareness allows for us to know exactly what values we have, which ones we want to obtain, and which ones we want to leverage.

It is imperative that we leverage our values in order to bring everything that we can to the table in each of our interactions.

Know your worth. This is probably something that you have heard over and over again throughout your lifetime. And I want to reiterate it here. It is important to know your worth; to know what you deserve, and to know what you can bring to the table. And knowing your worth or your value comes with self-awareness.

In my life, it is important for me to know that I am providing value and that I am valued. If I ever get to a point where I realize that I am not valued or that I am not providing value, then I know that it is time to walk away from a situation. This realization comes as a result of allowed awareness. I say allowed, because it is easy to close our eyes to that which we do not wish to see. However, you must not allow yourself to be blind to your situation. You should be able to ascertain what position you should be in at work as a result of what you know you can do. You should also be able and willing to be real with yourself and ask the hard questions. In order for me to be real with you here, this may come off harsh. But that is not my intention. My goal is to ask you to think about these hard questions because they are integral components to your individual growth. Ask yourself: Am I being compensated enough? Am I being overcompensated? Am I still bringing something to the table? Can I modify what I am bringing to the table to be of value? And then be honest with your reply. This honesty with yourself is the hard part. The best advice I can give you to achieve this degree of honesty with yourself is to stick to the facts and listen. Recognize if appealing factors (financial gain, for example) are veiling your truth and take the appropriate action. Let the proper factors persuade you.

Now, let me ask you: What is the purpose of staying if you cannot contribute to the team? What is the purpose of staying if your team is not valuing your worth? What is the purpose of staying if your goals are not in line with your company's? To be frank, there is no purpose other than to collect a paycheck or to say that you have a certain status. In my mind, that converts to greed, entitlement, a lack of integrity, and a void in your ability for self-awareness. Yes, you can try to troubleshoot and find other ways to be of value, but at some point, you also need to recognize when the needs of your company go beyond what you can provide to them (or vice versa).

I think this brings up an interesting question: What is value? Yes, value is the importance, worth, or usefulness of something, but it is also more than that. The true meaning of value is in the eyes of the beholder. The way that I view value may be different than the way that you view value. Why? Because the values that your practice and passion requires of you, may be different than the ones that mine require of me. Value is constantly transforming and evolving; it is something that oscillates and fluctuates depending on factors such as circumstance, position, and industry. Different circumstances, positions, and industries have different requirements, and as a result, value takes on varied meanings. These meanings should not equate value to compensation but rather to what you can bring to the table.

For example, in the early days, technologists could say that they provide value by building everything. Later on, the way that you provide value morphs, at least it did for me. I provided value by being a champion for people and for the culture so that we were so diligently looking to build.

In my mind, the only way that you can define yourself in an organization is by the value that you bring to it. As companies grow and more people are added to the team it is easy to feel as though you are not as integral to the functioning of the team because you can delegate a lot of what you had been responsible for in the past. If you focus on what you have always done as opposed to how you can provide value in the current ecosystem, you will have a hard time being an entrepreneur.

As CTO, I was always asking myself, "What should

the CTO of an organization of this size be doing?" My favorite answer I received when I asked people who had been in my position was "whatever needs to be done." In the early days, that usually entailed locking myself in a room and coding for fourteen hours a day. Later on, as I hired more developers to handle those tasks, that shifted the focus more to finding the right people to hire and ensuring that our culture didn't suffer from our rapid growth. Once we got past the point where we had the right team in place to hire and maintain our culture, my value shifted once again to being an advocate and sharing with as many people as possible what great things our organization was accomplishing. Value is a moving target, but as long as you can evaluate, "How can I provide value?" and then act accordingly, you are on the right track.

Eventually, I got to a point where I stopped providing the degree of value that I wanted to. I was not locked away coding, I was not championing our culture, and I was no longer advocating. The company was going one way and I was consciously starting to go another. And, I allowed myself to recognize this. That is the key.

My advice to you is this: be so self-aware that you can recognize when your skills equate to your perceived value, not your true value. Your perceived value is based on assumptions, not facts. If we are not fully and appropriately valued, our growth will be stunted and so too will our personal evolution.

I had found myself in a strange place where I wanted to grow in one direction, and Baker was already growing in another. What I mean is that I did not want to grow in the way that I could have grown (or needed to grow) had I decided that I really wanted to stay at Baker. This was not out of malice or laziness, but rather a function of wanting something different than I was getting (and different than I was going to be able to get).

This is something that happens often to founders in the entrepreneurial space. And when the path of the individual diverges from that of the company, it can be a result of the individual wanting something different for his or her own personal growth.

Now, it is important for me to mention that there are two sides of this. Given the option, some people will stay, despite the fact that the growth of their company does not resonate with what they want. Others will leave. The bigger questions become: Why do some people stay? How do you walk away from something that you built? How do you let yourself know that it is time to leave? Now, these are all big-picture questions, and I know that I cannot speak for everyone. But what I can tell you is what I think. I think that some people stay because they don't want to do anything else or because they are comfortable with the paycheck and their current status. And some people stay for reasons outside of the ones mentioned here.

Finding solutions to the last two questions requires some serious introspection. Throughout your journey, it is important for you to constantly self-reflect and assess the degree to which you are aligned with what you are doing within your company. If you begin to find that you are overwhelmed, unhappy, or misaligned, it is time to find a solution, and that solution might very well be change. This can be hard to accept at first, especially if you are finding yourself diverging internally from a company that you built (and subsequently poured years of your time and passion into). We become emotionally invested in the things that we build. The world of business does not leave room for emotions and in these circumstances neither should we. I have learned that it is possible to be honest with yourself and more so than that it is imperative. There is no secret formula for this, you just need to do it and be willing to listen to yourself.

If you ever end up at this place where you feel like it's time for you to walk down a different path, you may be wondering how you got here in the first place. How could something that was once so symbiotic transform into something that is hardly synergistic at all? What I can say is this: don't think too much about it. This is something that happens. You are human. You are constantly evolving, and what you want will fluctuate based on your own evolution.

I know how it goes. In the beginning, you and your company are often growing together, thriving as a result of your relationship to one another. However, when you stop growing (because your goals have shifted), the symbiosis stops, and therefore the growth and the value stop (for both you and your company). When this happens, you need to allow yourself to see that it is no longer the opportunity that it once was and that staying where you are only hinders your chance for more opportunity.

In a lot of ways, it is like a romantic relationship. You meet someone, you grow together, you learn together, and sometimes you just grow apart. You get to a point where the learning stops, where you have nothing else to offer, and you can stay and miss out on meeting a partner more suited for you and your needs—or you can leave and seek what else is out there.

Walking away from something that you poured your entire self into is not always easy, but there is no point in staying if you are no longer growing. Life is all about learning, changing, and elevating yourself. If you are in a similar position to the one that I am describing here (and there is no potential for growth), you are better off walking away, regardless of whether or not you are gaining something (such as a paycheck).

To me, this internal conflict became a matter of integrity. I felt that my impact had achieved its top weight.

I was no longer as effective to the company and therefore I was not as effective to my own journey. Yet, I was collecting a larger and larger paycheck. I got to a point at Baker where I was in a leadership position, doing just as much if not less than the people who worked under me, and yet I was making substantially more than they were. I could not get this to resonate with me. I felt as though they should be better compensated for their time and effort. I kept thinking, my salary is taking "x" amount away from the company, and my value is not increasing. What does that say about my leadership to this organization? In the end, the math did not add up to me, and I knew that I needed to walk away. This realization played an active role in my decision to seek growth through a different vector. As I said, it become an integrity thing, and for me this is of the utmost importance. No matter what I do, at the end of the day, I want to say that I have my integrity intact.

I am not the kind of person to think that I have "earned" something or that I deserve something as a result of my position or of the work that I have put in. In my mind, we are all working and we should all be compensated fairly for that labor regardless of whether we built the company or not. Just because you are at the top does not mean that you deserve what you are getting, especially if you are not working like you once did. Yes, I worked hard in the beginning to build Baker but that was the past. In the end, I did not resonate with the tasks that got me my paycheck.

I told you before, the money does not drive me, and I didn't choose this line of work just to cash a paycheck. I think if you go in with the mentality that you are doing what you want to do, the idea of staying for a paycheck holds a lesser value. And if you plan for this evolution, then you have the flexibility to leave.

I think that there is something to be said for what is fair and what is right and just. I think that there is money to go around and that when you get to a point when you do not feel that your value equates to your compensation, you should either walk away or try to make yourself more of an asset. Your value does not always equate to your salary.

If you choose to stay in a particular position past the point of diminishing returns, you are not only in a position of questionable integrity, you are also letting other potential opportunities pass you by, opportunities that could help you grow.

I think often about founders and other individuals who are part of the early stages of companies. For example, let's say that you were the twentieth employee at Facebook and you are still there. At this point in your career, you are making millions of dollars. You have money, you have access, and naturally you have an opportunity for growth.

Yet, you can't leave. Why? Because you have become accustomed to a specific level of income. You know that it is unlikely that you will go anywhere else and achieve that same level of income without sacrificing years only to get back to the point you are at now. Don't get me wrong, I can understand this mentality. I nearly fell prey to it. But, how much money do we really need? Why does it seem to be the only thing that fuels us? How do we get so comfortable with the cash flow that we fail to reach our own potential?

We end up in this position because we allow ourselves to. As you evolve in your career, keep your eyes wide open and be honest with yourself. Know your worth and stay true to yourself. Allow yourself to see what you would prefer to turn a blind eye to. When the growing stops, move on and find the next open door.

LET'S USE OUR HEADS
by MARVIN WASHINGTON

Marvin Washington is what legends are made of. Eleven seasons in the NFL, from the New York Jets, to the Denver Broncos, to the San Francisco 49ers, Marvin dominated the world of professional football with a passion and talent that few do, leaving an indelible mark on the game that continues to impact the lives of players even today. Yet it wasn't only his athleticism that shifted the paradigm of how we view the pinnacle of the human body and competition, it was his understanding that the body is fallible. When the world celebrates athletes as gods, the perception of immortality ironically becomes their Achilles Heel, and ultimately, a degeneration of their minds and bodies.

Heroes don't need medicine, they just need glory. Behind locker room doors, off the field, athletes are prescribed copious amounts of quick-cures that mask the extensive damage that players suffer in their trade-craft. Neurological and bodily injuries plague athletes on a mass scale, both during and after their careers, yet the cure is addiction. Those who bootstrap their way up the career ladder, based purely on grit and ferocious dedication are often the progeny of underserved minority communities, and as they move from rags to riches, their journey becomes one from a victim of the War on Drugs to victims of the professional pharmaceutical empires.

Had I not been as lucky as I am, I too would have been the prisoner of pharmaceuticals that the NFL pushed on my peers. It was my chance encounter with cannabis that became my helmet against the injuries of my sport. This plant - through a rigorous combination of scientific quantification and consumer use - has proven to time and again combat the depth of injury that athletes sustain. As a preventative measure, they reduce inflammation. As a post-injury antidote, if offers immediate therapeutic benefits. As a recreational tool, it offers a calmer and more cogent mind.

Cannabis has been used by our forefathers for generations before being villanized for the same reasons that our minority populations are: theirs, and our value poses an inherent risk to the status quo.

But closed head injuries are the result of closed-mind mentalities. To open minds, we have to expand our horizons, and nothing is more powerful for minority communities than emerging industries that combat generational stigmas, oppression with penal systems, and an institutionalized lack of wellness. This industry is still in its infancy, and the opportunity to advance its impact on medicine and minds is unparalleled.

I want to be successful, see this plant offer an equitable shot for all, and share my truth. To me, success means that twenty years from now, people will be at their best - in sport, in health, and in society. As leaders in cannabis, we are simply temporary placeholders, setting the table for future generations to come. That is what I am trying to do. I want to be a role model for other minorities. I want others to see their value, and that of their health. Perhaps most importantly, I want everyone to live their goals, on and off the field.

CHAPTER 6

HCD

Is the highest common denominator an altruistic quest?
Depends on how you view altruism. I think of it as a
marker of an ideal, something that we can aspire to.
What is its value? It aligns minds to serve a better self,
and in turn, a better cause. What is its obligation? To
hold ourselves accountable as we climb the ladder of self-
progress in achieving goals that augment the quality of our
world. Success is shared.
The question is why – why share this now, and to what
end? For years, i practiced the unnamed practice of self-
elevation in both business and personal settings. As any
minority can attest, being taken seriously in a business
environment is set to a much higher standard – meaning,
professionalism is dotting your "i's" and crossing your
"t's" in just the right way. You must be that much more
professional, that much more attentive, and just that much
more willing to sacrifice.
This pressure cooker is the petri dish in which the concept
of the HCD simmered and evolved. The cannabis
industry is suffering the same disproportionate treatment
– not being taken seriously by so many of the stakeholders
whose barometer is completely skewed. The industry is
still, despite its growth, value, and revenue, is still being
tethered to outdated notions in business circles. So what is

the solution? Fighting against this unfair and unproductive
treatment requires elevating the conversation – essentially,
intersecting at the highest common denominator. Setting the
highest standards means we need to be, and do better than
any other industry just to arrive at a level playing field.
The onus is on us – and if we accept the responsibility of
setting the right baselines, the world, our industry, and its
impact will be better for it.

***

Meet at the Highest Common Denominator
highest common denominator
/highest common denominator/
noun

the most sophisticated point of intersection between two
or more people

The highest common denominator is a principle
born of mutualism, of iterative growth, and of a
willingness to heighten yourself and your abilities. Now,
this does not mean that to elevate yourself you need
to interact with someone who has the same exact life
experiences as you do. All it means is that you need to be
willing to bring everything that you have to the table in a
conversation aimed at reconciling commonalties, and your

counterpart must be willing to do the same. Now, as you know, it is extraordinarily rare to cross paths with someone whose understanding of the world is parallel, or a mirror of your own outlook. We all differ in our approach, and in our expectations of situations. So, what you must do is you must seek the "shared" between you and another individual and that commonality is where you begin to intersect.

The highest common denominator is not personal - it does not belong to us. It is not mine, nor is it yours. It is a baseline and in every interaction, you should seek to elevate from that starting point. Now, I don't want you to think of a baseline as something that is low, because in this case the baseline is one that you have designed, curated, and most importantly, chosen as a function of creating opportunity. It is the highest, greatest level of something. And anything that brings this baseline higher is simply an augmentation of an already incredible mindset.

We are all individuals with different thoughts, desires, and life experiences. What I know to be true is different than what you know to be true, or relevant, and for us to intersect at the HCD, we need to speak the same language. To do this, I try to contextualize my interactions. For example, if I know that you are someone who likes science, I might try to break down the technicalities of my tech-talk to match what I think that you know. The art of intersection requires that you become an active speaker, and an intentional listener. Practically, I try and use metaphors that contextualize my language, and I am most engaged when others can do the same. When communities and individuals can speak a common language, we aren't losing what is shared in an attempt at translation. This contextualization is key to intersecting at the HCD and to provide this context you must strive to understand the person in front you, and most importantly, you must employ a wide breadth of knowledge. Earlier, we covered why it is better to know a decent amount about a lot of things than it is to know everything about one thing in social situations. The more you know, the more you can relate to people and then the more likely you are to elevate yourself and another person in an interaction. Also, remember what you don't know, and continue to be willing to learn. There is always something to be gained by admitting that you might simply not know.

I cannot help but mention humility - a characteristic that is essential to an interaction with the HCD. Asking questions and demonstrating humility is just as important as gathering knowledge. Asking questions and saying that you do not know will make the space where you intersect a safe one. This safe space will facilitate even more growth.

Grow, iterate, evolve.

The success that we had at Baker, even, was a result

of intersecting at the HCD. Joel, David, and I each came in with varying skill sets. My strength was not David's strength and Joel's strength was neither mine nor David's strength. Yet, we intersected at our differences. Each time we interacted, no matter the topic, it was at the highest level of thought, and what we brought to the table became a matter of both educating, and learning. So, while all of our strengths were not in the same arena, our values were in line with one another. The balance we found between our strengths and values allowed us to be as successful as we were. The HCD of our company was the area where each of our strengths, values, and skill sets could intersect. And, our product is proof of that. The platform we built is a tangible manifestation of the combination of each of these things. Without the intersection that results from our interactions, this product and this company would not be successful. It was each of our parts that made it a whole.

As we have discussed, it is important to know your value so that you can know exactly what you can bring to the table. If you know your value, your strength, and your skillset you can use simple introspection to decipher what it is that you may still need to achieve your version of success. By knowing not just what you have, but also what you don't have, you can achieve more. To do this, you must be willing to swallow your ego and admit what it is that you may "lack." In the end, you will be more successful in life and business if you can do this. I say life, because while you may be able to find what you "lack" in another person, you may also be able to find it in yourself. Now, this is not true for all things. For example, I can draw, and my degree reflects that skill, but I am not on the level of some artists and even with a load of classes and high level intersections I may never be at that level. I know this, I acknowledge this, and if I need an artist, I will seek one out. Some may call this delegation, and it is true, but the truth is, I know that my inclinations sometimes cannot reconcile with my needs, and so, I learn that my hopeful talents aren't applicable in every arena. But again, that does not mean that I cannot work on my drawing skills in the meantime. Run your own cost/benefit analysis and you'll find the same is true of many other traits that simply can't be leveraged in a professional environment.

As I talk about leveraging values and skill sets, I cannot help but think about the avatars in "World of WarCraft" that have bars that represent each of the character's strengths. To build the strongest troop, it is wise to pick players with varying strengths. This eliminates the potential for weakness because there is an expert in each area. To build your tribe, you must do the same. Identify the varying strengths of the members of your tribe and leverage them for your success. You do not need the same subset of knowledge as your conversational counterpart to intersect at the HCD – teaching, learning, humility, and contextualizing are all part of meeting at a higher plane.

We can gain something from each and every interaction. But, to truly gain something of substance, you have to intersect at the highest level possible. The point I am getting at here is that in every interaction, I want you to try to think about the ways in which you can add to what you already know. What can you learn that can help to increase your value and build your skillset? How can you share your value to help someone else to build their skillset? Know that you are seeking to go above the baseline and look to leave each interaction with more heightened knowledge than you entered it with.

Heightened interactions oftentimes require a degree of processing. For some people this processing may begin to happen in person while the interaction is taking place. For others this processing may happen at home during moments of quiet and intentional introspection. Neither option is better or worse than the other and regardless of which type of introspection is best suited to you, the fact that you are engaging in this mindful practice is proof that you achieved your target intersection as you conversed. If you find that this is the case, you have certainly aligned at the HCD – this introspection and elevation from an interface is the product of having met at the highest common denominator. These powerful interactions push you to be better than you were before and the introspection that occurs helps to push you to new heights. Remember, the more you know, the more you can do.

Now, these conversations of higher thought do not only happen in the workplace, they can happen anywhere. But, I should mention, a significant conscious effort is required to intersect at the highest level and it is not realistic for every single interaction in your life to be at the level of the HCD. Sometimes, you are just tired, or you are at Starbucks and the guy cashing you out is talking about the weather. To be clear, talking about the weather is not an interaction that occurs at the HCD. A talk about the weather would be an example of intersecting at the lowest common denominator (LCD). More often than not, it can be a waste of time. But, every now and then it is okay to meet at the LCD, pleasantries are a part of life after all - just make sure the line behind you at Starbucks isn't too long! The reality here is that you will need to pick and choose where and how you intersect. Could you interact at the HCD with the guy talking about the weather and elevate the conversation to something else? Sure. But, is it a good use of your time? Probably not but it just depends on the day.

You need to weigh the opportunity of choosing to intersect at the HCD. I am not telling you to judge a book by its cover, I am telling you to know where you are mentally on any given day. If you assess that you have the energy to intersect at the HCD, do it. There is an opportunity to intersect with nearly anyone at this level – both parties just must be willing.

So, why should we do this? Why should we intersect at the HCD? What really is the goal of this? The goal is the HCD is to live your best life. In my opinion, doing this requires that you never stop improving and that you consistently help others to improve as well. If you are intersecting at the HCD, then you are getting closer to the best version of your life everyday by continuing to intersect at the highest level possible. By intersecting at the HCD, you are also helping others to live their best life. This is an act of service. Put another way, your genuine input and ability to contextualize a conversation with the goal of elevating yourself and another person is a qualifier for living your best life.

Life is a matter of give and take, and as you take from these intersections my hope is of course that you would then continue to give and pay it forward. As you pay it forward, imagine how many other people that you intersect with will pay it forward. Imagine then, that this manner of speaking could spread throughout a community, throughout your tribe. I am sure you can ascertain that the highest common denominator can transcend small interactions and become a commonality within a community. So, imagine then what could happen when your community intersects with another community. What would happen?

By elevating yourself, you elevate your tribe, which elevates other tribes. This goal is built on the idea that deep down, we all want to be the best version of ourselves. We all want to live our best lives, whether we admit it or not; and this intersection is your ticket. Just think about what we could accomplish in a world where everyone sought to impart knowledge, do research, and interact with others at the most sophisticated levels of thought. The limits would be endless.

Like I said, I used the HCD to get where I am today. The first time that I was required to intersect at a level higher than the one that I knew was at Duke. My acceptance into the university was the exception to their rule, and I did everything in my power to mask that. I intentionally surrounded myself with people whose ideals matched my own and I leveled up. I shared values and my skill sets with them and took what I could for each of my interactions. I become stronger because of this. By the time I graduated, I was on the level of my fellow classmates. I had risen from my circumstance.

After graduation, I set my sights on my profession. As you might remember I spent many years working in consulting and start-ups. Each one of these encounters forced me to level up. So, I did, and again I took what I could, knowing that I was more elevated than I had been when I started.

By the time the opportunity to start Baker came around, I harnessed a myriad of values and skill sets that came from years of sophisticated and intentional intersections. I had jumped through hoops and been exposed to many new ideas. Because of this I had everything that I needed to align with Joel and David. As we intersected, we created a product that had never existed before, something so great that breaking it down was inconceivable. What we built was transformative. It was a product of the HCD and more so than that it was a product that will always be remembered. A product born of complementary skill sets and of elevated mindsets. A product born of pioneers who wanted to pave the way for change.

As Baker grew, so did I. Each calculated change that occurred for the betterment of the company influenced me and ultimately transformed the way the world interacts with the plant. What we created helped the world to see the plant in a different light. It helped the world see the science, the options, and the potential. I want to say that as the industry evolved, Baker's model of diversity and market-facing solutions helped alter the perception of the industry to a new stratosphere. As cannabis changed, evolving from the constraints of its backyard, so too did I.

Optionality is the future
optionality
/optionality/
noun

the quality of being available to be chosen but not obligatory

The cannabis industry has been constantly shifting and elevating since our society began to entertain the idea of federal legalization. The rapidity of this conversation - from conception to current day - is barely a decade. Yet the industry - our ideas, our innovations, our visions - had to work at warp speed to match the fever pitch of the new potential of our industry. An example: chain dispensaries were not in existence and their storefronts only served persons with medical cards. If you wanted cannabis back in 2004, you called it weed, and you bought it illegally off of a dealer. Consumption was taboo and frowned upon. Anything that you sought to learn on the topic came from first-hand experience with the plant. When your friends rolled a joint, you did not ask whether it was indica or sativa, you simply inhaled. Business then was not like business now. Business was done behind closed doors, with guns strapped to belts. Product was sold on the illicit market. Today, the industry has morphed from crossed arms and bro hugs to ties and handshakes. Times are different.

Now, fifteen years later we are in the age of sophistication, exiting the bridge of adolescence that carried us away from the days of underground grows. We are watching the commoditization of cannabis. While cannabis still awaits federal legalization in the US, it has been legalized at the state level and this has allowed for unprecedented amounts of trial, experimentation, innovation, and evolution. The legal market, no matter how small or novel has created a wave of change that will continue to flow through the market. And the most exciting part? We are still only at the beginning. At this point, smaller businesses have been faced with the decision of aligning with the market or getting out of the way. Those who have decided to align, have likely been met with some sort of reward. The infancy of this legal market created room for growth that never before existed. They leveled up. They followed the rules. Really people in this industry or people coming into it have three choices: lead, follow, or get out of the way.

This space is filled with opportunity for entrepreneurs and today, the risk is not quite what it was. Whether that is directly correlated to the reward, we won't know just yet, only time will tell.

I was part of the first generation of entrepreneurs in the legal cannabis space. My generation was the first who came into this space, noted the risk, and proceeded anyway. Today, we are seeing the second generation of entrepreneurs come into the space. This group that did not have the risk tolerance that my generation did. They wanted to see the aftermath of companies such as mine— they wanted to see that our exits could be successful. They saw our success and they marched in. Risk tolerance aside, this new generation, like the many that will follow have something to provide this space (so long as they are intersecting at the HCD and playing by the rules). This group is determined, sophisticated, innovative, and ready to build on the foundation that we set.

In my opinion, this is where the HCD comes in. The HCD comes in during generational and cross-generational interactions where we can seek to elevate one another. Regardless of when we entered into the industry, we each have something to offer one another, we each have the ability to help the person next to us live their best life, and in turn, we have an opportunity to live our own. As the industry grows, the ego should not replace a willingness to share knowledge. We should meet at the contextualized baseline of the HCD and combine our innovative powers for the greater good of the future. This potentiality is limitless. Intersecting at the HCD is a matter of awareness and a matter of upholding the values that have for so long been associated with success.

As the industry grows, we really need to take a good hard look at the value system that we seek to uphold and this should be the standard for the people who seek to elevate this space. While there has been progress, there is still room for exponential growth in this space. There are still long-standing ideals and prejudices that need to be broken and rebuilt to continually transform this ever-changing industry and it is more than possible that such a transformation can occur.

Without a principle such as the HCD encouraging high level interactions, it is quite probable that the metric by which we measure value can drop below what we desire. Our goal as an industry should be to continue to elevate exponentially off of the baseline.

In order for this to happen we each need to be responsible not just for our groups, but for ourselves. We must uphold our own values sets and strive to always put our best foot forward.

The question then is this: How do you define value in an industry that is still defining itself? How do you define yourself in an industry where the metric is arbitrary? I think you do this by aligning with values that have worked well with other industry. The values should exude professionalism, a strong desire to succeed, humility, and ambition for a better future. Our society has already set a standard of what we could consider to be professional and successful. We have established a way to speak, to dress, to carry ourselves. That very image must be something that carries over to the cannabis industry if we are to be taken seriously. Like I said, if you want to compete, you need to play by the rules and big business has rules.

There is an exciting period of discovery ahead of us as we face federal legalization. Such a ruling would allow scientists to conduct the research that we have long been waiting for. All I keep thinking is that we won't know what we don't have until the research is conducted. I think that this research is going to open the doors for even more modalities of interactions with the plant. It will allow us to truly get the answers of how the plant works and its long-term effects on the body. In turn, we will likely be able to find more uses for cannabis than we already know of. So, while we don't know what the future is, what I can imagine is that there are countless vectors and possibilities for growth. These vectors and possibilities will create more pathways which in turn creates even more options. At the end of all of this there is optionality, which reinforces why I got into this industry in the first place. Yes, I see opportunity because I seek it and because I want to see it. We have established that. But when I say that there is potential in this industry what I am really talking about is the very optionality that allowed me to interact with this industry in the first place.

I am not a cultivator of the plant. As you may remember from earlier chapters, I consumed the plant as a result of a lifestyle choice. I enjoyed it and I was baffled by the negative connotations associated with it. After consuming the plant, I held a firm belief that we should be given the option to choose whether or not we consume. And my stance on optionality has not changed since. I want to be clear, this optionality is something that transcends consumption and can exist in different vectors of life. But, what I love most about the cannabis industry is the very fact that there are unlimited pathways, some still unexplored, for the entrepreneur to find opportunity. I have a technology background and because of this I found my niche and I laid down a slate for other entrepreneurs who may be on the other side of the industry, such as scientists or cultivators. This industry has a space for you whether it be peripheral, and market based or completely plant based. You can claim your stake no matter who you are, and this is what I love the most.

The reason I did not get into the industry in 2005 had a lot to do with how I qualify opportunity. By now I am sure you can guess that I qualify an opportunity by the available optionality and the inherent value that my choice could bring to me (and that I could bring for it). I would not have been of value back in 2005. Not to mention, this optionality that I speak of today, did not exist back then. But it did when I got in, and it does now more than ever. There was a space for me when I got in and there is a space for you now, no matter who you are, so long as you are willing to elevate yourself.

This industry provides optionality in a way that industries have never been able to and this excites me as we stand on the edge of the future. I cannot help but smile at the wave of entrepreneurs entering into this space – the ones who innovate, who play by the rules, and build upon the foundation that was leveraged and transformed by David, Joel, and myself.

Know your potential and there will always be a path
potential
/potential/
adjective

having or showing the capacity to become or develop into something in the future

So, you did it. You made it. You climbed the seemingly never-ending stairwell and you made it to the top. You reached your goals. You defined success. And now, you have everything that you ever thought you wanted, but there is still something inside of you, something urging you forward. You ate, but you are still hungry. You don't know what it is that is making you want more. But you have time to think about it; maybe too much time. So, what do you do?

I am going to be honest here. I have absolutely no idea. Your guess is as good as mine.

I got where I wanted to go. I became successful within the framework that I both created and defined for myself. And now I find myself filled with questions that I have never asked before. From a young age, I always had a myopic sense of direction that was steered by my vision of success. I knew I wanted to attend a top university. I knew that I wanted to work for myself. I knew that I wanted to build a company. I did all of those things. And now that I have done everything that I ever wanted to, I have no idea where to go. So, I have to redefine the next step of my journey.

I find myself constantly pondering not just what to do next, but the point of it all. Why do we dare to dream? And what is the point of chasing what we want? What is the point of any endeavor for that matter? Why are we filled with this need to build, to grow, to attempt? And here again, I do not have answers for you. Like I said, for the first time in my life these are spaces that I cannot seem to fill – answers awaiting solutions. Right now, I feel as though I am stumped and hardly beginning to write the proof.

For the first time, I am free. I am free to be whoever I want to be. I am free to do whatever I want. I keep asking questions. Who do I want to be next? What is the point of this evolved self that I have created? And is this evolved self not just a new base? I feel like I am sitting on top of a cliff with wings; I have the ability to fly; but, the weight of the uncertainty is weighing me down.

The unknown is not something that I have ever considered to be daunting. Part of me has always embraced it, but I had always been walking on some path that I had carved out for myself – so while it may have looked dark in the distance, I was too occupied with tasks in front of me, tasks that I knew would make the dark distance a little bit lighter. The unknown that I face now is different. The uncertainty seems more daunting, perhaps because I know of the potential that it may hold.

Sometimes I cannot imagine what could top my experience with Baker. I cannot imagine what will trump the pride and fulfillment that consumed me. What will the shape of fulfillment look like? What will it feel like? And what will the next evolved version of myself look like? And how do I find meaning when I am no longer a part of what was one of the most meaningful experiences in my life? Again, so many questions and so few answers; questions that I know that I need to ask myself in order to take my next step.

In all of this uncertainty, I know a few things for sure. My past will always be a part of me. Baker will always be a part of me. The relationships I formed during my time there will always be a part of me. I know that I am not comfortable with the status quo. And I never feel settled with stagnancy – like I said earlier, I am not one who is able to stand still. So, while I wait for the next step to illuminate, I know this – as soon as I find my direction I am going to keep climbing. There is no chance that I will put my hand to the railing and begin walking down the staircase that I worked so hard to climb. I know that opportunity is out there and with it, there is potential. I also know of the potential that exists inside of me and as I find what is next, I will seek to stretch it, to expand it, to see just what I am capable of next. I know that my potential is unlimited and as for my future, the sky is the limit.

OPTICS
by RICO TARVER

Rico Tarver is a leader, enthusiast, and a man of conviction whose work in cannabis opened his eyes to the value of health and passion that comes with work. His efforts as a Tedx speaker, emcee, host, and consultant has given him all the experience to be the leader and trendsetter he is today. He is listed as one of the High Times Magazine "100 Most Influential People."

Why did I get into cannabis?

To stay alive.

It wasn't more complicated than that, or more dramatic. I just had to stay focused.

The system isn't set up to help you win - especially if you look a certain way. You grow up without a lot, and so you start idealizing the shit that is supposed to fill you up.

But it's draining.

You set up desires. You use your talents. You rely on your skills. Even then, you end up on the fringes of what you thought you'd be. You make compromises - hell, you make justifications - for why selling out isn't giving up - it is the buy in you need to prove your worth.

Who are we proving it too, though? Who placed a value on us that we keep trying to raise? I was treated like my value was worthless.

Cannabis was the only one, the only industry, the only community, that made me feel priceless.

And so, I raised the bar. I give back - in sweat, in hustle, in balls - what this industry gave me. It gave me health. A chance at life. Respect. Value. Worth.

But to get here, I had to forge a path. No one had laid out the way. I used every dollar, every opportunity, every ounce of grit to get up and sell. I learned that hustling doesn't mean selling an eighth or selling out - it means selling yourself. It means rising to the challenge, battling your demons, and focusing on what has always mattered.

But life didn't send me on an easy path. It forced changes in me until I transformed. To go higher, I sunk real low.

I have lived three different lives.

In my first one, I was the son of a military family, and moved around the world until finally settling in the Northeast. I was a smart kid who played football. I got a scholarship, went to a prestigious university, and was on track for success.

That life ended the day I ruptured my achilles.

My second life started the day I was prescribed the

opioids to deal with the pain during recovery. I became a secret addict, and being an intimidating looking black man (whatever that means), I couldn't even find a job despite my education. To survive, I sold weed on the streets of Chicago across from Wrigley Field, and bounced at a club to make ends meet. There was no glamour in it either – I hustled because it fed my opioid addiction. I was disillusioned and desperate, but addiction has a way of keeping you depressed enough to feed it, and nothing else. I functioned, but barely, until the day that I landed a job in the white world of corporate finance. I even tried to be the anti-establishment guy amidst the buttoned up suits – but that didn't deter them. To them, I was a black hire with a knack for sales. And so, I sold out – dreams, ethics, and health. I witnessed firsthand the total lack of ethics in that industry. I chased the wrong green, and so, I got cash rich, and character poor.

That life ended the day I found a tumor in my neck.

My third life started the day that I was reintroduced to cannabis. I learned how to properly utilize the plant to curb my opioid use, and within 6 months, had completely beat my addiction. Luckily, my tumor was benign, but my mortality - my purpose, my character, my legacy - suddenly those urgencies fired me up. I had to make a change, and make it last. The grass seemed green, and so, I chased that.

That life led me to where I am today – an advocate, voice, and energizer of an industry that gave me a second chance to realize my potential, and then launch it. I was attracted, ok, I was addicted, to the chaos of the challenge - it was a high to see how high I could climb, but I was finally thinking clearly.

It wasn't easy though – in fact, I had to use every creative tool, every ounce of commitment, and my life savings to launch myself into the newly legalizing California market.

I had to drive, walk, knock and talk my way to success.

But what I continue to learn, is that no man is an island. You gotta level up if you want to meet the minds who shape worlds. I was lucky enough to have met a guy, who knew a guy.

The guy who opened the door to this opportunity, was Roger. Arm around my shoulder, out for a drink, walking me into a chance at success that reconciled my passion with my skills. When I was hired at Baker Technologies, I had one job: sell, sell, sell. I had very few tools – most of which I had to sharpen – but I possessed one trait that ultimately raised my expectations – charm. I knew that sales wasn't about picking up the phone and hoping I got through. It was about knocking on doors, building relationships, and adding to an ecosystem. For the first time, I saw color in power – black and brown faces that hustled for a cause – and this irony wasn't lost on me. For generations, we suffered the injustice of the laws designed to oppress us. Cannabis was both our ticket into, and now our ticket out of the manufactured criminality of weed. The industry opened a chance for brilliant minds – from women, from minorities, from poor folks – to get a foothold into a better life. I had a story to tell, and I knew that countless others did too.

So, I walked the length and width of California hearing the stories of founders, of growers, of thinkers. I heard passion, and health, and justice.

From the finance world – where cocaine was expected but cannabis was shunned – meaning, where health was unimportant and optics were everything – to this industry, where smoke and mirrors gets you tossed out - I aligned. To gain the respect of my peers, I couldn't bullshit. I had to be authentic, and to be real, I had to realize how much was, and is, at stake.

I infiltrated the system by helping change the rules – bringing each other up means putting a megaphone in the faces of activists and companies that put their money where their mouth is. Validating their passion for the industry meant being inclusive, and that one act on the first day I met Roger – that one act of taking the time to include me in the conversation – that was my litmus test for everyone else that I worked with from that point forward.

Now is the time to get up, stand up for something, and shout. I learned to play defense, and thrive in the chaos of a time that the efforts of one of the most diverse industries in the world will ultimately change the lives of everyone who desires a better one.

This life – this life that lives because of the plant – this is the life I was always meant to live.

EPILOGUE

Elevating society is your responsibility
society
/society/
noun

a community, or broad grouping of people having common traditions, institutions, and collective activities and interests formed to achieve common aims

I opened this narrative with a quote from Aristotle, "The worst form of inequality is to try and make unequal things, equal." There are many readings of this sentiment. My understanding was immediately apparent: society should not expect equal opportunity. Instead, it should demand equal access to opportunity. I have been the recipient of programs designed to catapult me into different, and higher echelons of society. I didn't align with that mentality then, and I don't align with it now. This isn't because I feel that programs shouldn't exist that open the doors of equality for all. It is because checking off boxes for merely the concept of inclusion is the worst form of infantilizing, mitigating, and pigeon-holing underserved and underrepresented segments of society. Those programs, organizations, and mindsets aimed at truly providing the resources, opportunities, and access to an elevated vantage point in life are often met with either a quota that they are allowed to fill or with promises of betterment that typically don't materialize.

We live in the most diverse and powerful nation on Earth, and frankly, we can do better.

Society's great equalizer can't be money; it must be success. What I mean is that if we aren't focused on the qualifying metrics of a fulfilled life and real optionality for all, and instead on quantifying which percentages of our culture are appropriated what proportions of opportunity, then we are failing at every level.

The symbiosis, the connection, the actual elevation of our society must be an intentional, actionable, and compelling intersection between the possessors of prospects, and the seekers of success.

I was always confused at the value social equity programs brought to my life. I was then further exasperated at the requirements placed on companies to meet their equity recipient quotas. I was then even further angered at the almost insulting and undignified process that many recipients of social equity programs were forced to endure once "placed" in a company – often given busy work instead of useful education.

I know this because I lived it.

To me, and Baker, diversity wasn't a demand – it was natural. We didn't hire to represent; we hired because it was representative of the intelligence, skills, and value that various people with varying life experiences brought.

I think of how my color-blindness was a secret weapon – I looked for the best, the hungriest, and the most willing.

I know that organizations are now rapidly attempting to diversify both their leadership and their teams. That is an important step. But reconciling attempt with action is the measure of real progress.

After my exit, I saw a door.

Upon walking through, I realized that the thousands of interactions that helped create my HCD were purpose driven to a powerful calling: dedicate my time, resources, network, skills, ambitions, passions, and knowledge to create a social conversation. By leveraging the years of learning, by transforming the lessons into tools, and by harnessing these tools to empower others, our world could rise above the lower and base differences that have plagued humanity for millennia.

Through action, we can achieve progress.

Through progress, we can elevate our society.

Through elevation, we can continue to aim higher.

We can meet at the top and create a new baseline for success.

I suggest we call it the Highest Common Denominator.

Made in the USA
Monee, IL
04 December 2019